BONITA BARRETT

ROCK STOCK

BONITA BARRETT

BONITA BARRETT

Copyright © 2024 Bonita Barrett

All rights reserved.

ISBN: 9798884627222

BONITA BARRETT

DEDICATION

For Evie, Charlie and Jamie. You are my sunshine.

ROCK STOCK

The Pockbury Times

FREE FOR POCKBURY RESIDENTS   WRITTEN BY MARK DOOLEY

ROCK STAR
WORLD EXCLUSIVE
WHERE HAS HE BEEN HIDING?

Music fans have been desperate to know what's happened to local legend Rock Star since his accident on New Year's Eve.

The world-famous musician, known for hits such as 'Rock My Paper Scissors' and 'Bats For Breakfast', was **rushed to hospital** from his nearby mansion and hasn't been seen since.

Rock Star was performing his well-known stage stunt - smashing his guitar over the piano and **chewing on the pieces**. Minutes later, the ageing rocker was hugging a Christmas tree, clutching his belly, and crying for his mum. Footage from the party was recently leaked on YouTube and has now been streamed over 100 million times.

After months of silence, the megastar finally contacted us to '**set the record straight**'. Rock Star revealed that his love of eating instruments came to a painful end that same night.

During a life-saving gastric operation, surgeons removed a record 36 instrument parts - along with Rock Star's **entire stomach**.

Known to many locals by his real name, Sid Shufflebottom, Rock Star has now been forced to change his partying ways for a lifestyle more suited to his real age (67).

Rock Star told us the hardest part about losing his stomach is living off a strict **soup-based diet**. "I love food, I've eaten it all my life. Now I've basically got a tube that runs from one set of cheeks to the other. That sucks, man. I miss eating, I miss chewing, and I miss proper food! Soup tastes like drinking a puddle!"

Now more 'Gastric Band' than 'Rock Band', Rock Star certainly hasn't '**got the guts**' for wild parties anymore. Is this finally the start of the end for our most famous resident?

CHAPTER 1 – THE CRAZY IDEA

Freddie never imagined that having a secret talent would be so complicated.

At first, Freddie had decided to keep his talent a secret because it wasn't very *cool*. Then, when everything happened last year, he *needed* to keep it a secret so that he didn't draw any extra attention to their little family. But after reading the article about Rock Star, everything had changed.

Right now, he wanted to run down the street and tell *everyone* about his secret talent, and most excitingly, what he was planning to do with it. The only problem was, Freddie couldn't. For his mum's sake, he had to blend into the background.

Fortunately for Freddie, *blending in* was easy. On the outside, he looked like an average 12-year-old boy – average height, average weight, average amount of teeth, even the average amount of spots. His scruffy brown hair, hazel eyes and ears that were slightly too big for his head didn't make him stand out in any way. But on the inside, he was far from average. Freddie Wilson was a *very* different 12-year-old indeed.

Freddie hadn't chosen his secret talent; it had chosen him. When his dad first died, Freddie spent hours in the garden sitting next to his dad's vegetable patch. Freddie could picture his dad there whenever he wanted, and it made him feel less sad. Dad's vegetable patch hadn't realised it didn't have a dad anymore, so the vegetables had carried on growing. Freddie soon found himself surrounded by all this new life, and he couldn't bear for his dad's hard work to go to waste. In that moment, the seeds of his talent had been planted.

He decided to teach himself how to cook everything that grew. Before long, he was experimenting and inventing new dishes. In the last two years, he'd become surprisingly good at it too.

While most kids his age were playing on the Xbox or

watching YouTube, Freddie was making mouthwatering meals and delicious desserts. While most kids dreamt of becoming famous footballers or viral YouTube sensations, Freddie dreamt of winning MasterChef and travelling the world, cooking for the rich and famous.

The only people that knew about Freddie's secret talent were his mum, his gran and his best friend Dylan. The three of them loved everything he created – except one. Soup. The most boring food on the planet. Freddie spent hours making the tastiest soups, but the only person that would try them was his gran… and that was only to give her false teeth a rest.

Freddie listened carefully for any signs of movement. The only sound was his mum's terrible singing drifting down the stairs as she worked. Nothing else. No footsteps, no creaky floorboards. His heart racing, he rested back against the front door and read the article again. This was it. This was his big chance.

Freddie knew that even though Rock Star lived just three miles away, their lives were worlds apart. Rock Star was world famous, he lived in a huge mansion, and he was a multimillionaire. Freddie wasn't noticed by anybody, he lived in a small semi-detached house with his mum and dog, and he had the grand total of £36 in his bank account.

But Freddie preferred to concentrate on what they had in common. They had both been born in Pockbury, and they both had a talent. Rock Star had used his talent to follow his dreams and travel the world, and Freddie had plans to do exactly the same.

Holding the newspaper in his hand, Freddie looked at his reflection in the mirror. He couldn't help wondering if the boy staring back at him had come up with a truly magnificent idea, or a *really* crazy one. There was only one way to find out.

Freddie ran through to the kitchen, grabbed his latest invention out of the oven and quickly placed the tray on the cooling rack. He threw on his shoes and crept down the garden to the broken fence panel he'd used a million times before. Freddie took a deep breath and squeezed through.

CHAPTER 2 - DYLAN

Dylan's family had moved next door when Freddie was three, and they'd been best friends ever since. Being four months older and having moved from Wales (which was a whole other country), Freddie knew his best friend had *much* more life experience.

Dylan was taller and wider than his friend. He had thick black hair, with rosy cheeks and big blue eyes. He also had an infectiously loud laugh.

Dylan loved making up strange sayings and turning words backwards, or *'backwords'* as Dylan liked to call them. As a big fan of sugar, Dylan loved Freddie's *stressed* - which is desserts spelled backwards. His favourites were *ekac* (cake), and *eci maerc* (ice cream). The cool thing was that with his Welsh accent, Dylan could make these things sounds like real words.

It didn't bother his mum and dad, probably because *mum* and *dad* are the same whichever way round, but it drove everyone else crazy – except Freddie. Dylan had one of those faces that meant Freddie could never stay angry at him.

As Freddie raced up the garden and into Dylan's kitchen, he was greeted by his best friend's bottom. The rest of him was wedged well and truly in the snack cupboard.

'You'll never guess what!' said Freddie, quickly followed by the thud of Dylan's head. Dylan reversed out carefully, fiercely rubbing his thick black hair.

'Burst my blisters,' cried Dylan, 'that hurt!'

Freddie held out the newspaper. 'Have you seen this?'

'Yeah, it's called a *newspaper*," replied Dylan, rolling his eyes. 'Old people read them.'

Freddie pointed at the front page. 'Mate, you need to read this!'

'This is worse than school,' muttered Dylan, rubbing his head and feeling through his thick black hair for a bump. When he finished reading, he scrunched up his face.

'Isn't it brilliant?' said Freddie.

Dylan looked confused. '*Rock Rats* having his insides removed is brilliant? I hope it never happens to me!'

'*You* don't eat guitars for breakfast like Rock Star,' said Freddie, 'besides, you're missing the point. I'm not saying it to be mean. It's the opposite. I want to help him!'

'Help him?' spluttered Dylan. 'How?'

'Rock Star's living off soup! This is it... my big chance to cook for someone famous!'

Dylan's mouth dropped open. 'Are you serious?'

'Why not?' asked Freddie.

Dylan shook his head in disbelief. 'Mate, this isn't like making tea for your gran!'

'I know *that*,' sighed Freddie, 'but I make loads of soup, and it's really tasty! It's daft chucking it, when Rock Star's having to *live* off the stuff. He might be famous, but he still needs to eat!'

'You're crazy!' said Dylan.

'But good crazy, yeah?'

'Well, you're forgetting a couple of things...'

'Like what?' asked Freddie.

Dylan held out his hand to count on his fingers. 'For starters, is *Rock Rats* really going to try something made by a kid?'

Freddie scrunched up his face. 'And the second?'

Dylan cringed. 'Your mum'.

CHAPTER 3 - THE PROBLEM

'Mum can't find out, that's for sure,' sighed Freddie, remembering the article about his mum on the front-page of the same newspaper last year. 'She's only just started leaving the house again. I'm still having to bin the paper every week, so she doesn't get upset.' Freddie dropped into a chair at the kitchen table.

'Oh well, it was a cool idea!' said Dylan, patting his friend on the back.

Freddie shook his head. 'What do you mean? I'm still doing it! I just can't tell her, that's all. She'd stress too much... and you know what happens then.'

Dylan shuddered, walked to the cupboard, pulled out the KitKat he'd managed to find earlier and snapped it in two. He handed half to Freddie.

'I tell you what,' said Freddie, pointing his chocolate bar in his friend's direction, 'this helps with *your* dream too!'

Dylan looked confused. 'How does *you* making soup for Rock Rats help *me* become a famous YouTuber?'

Freddie smiled. 'Because the sooner I start cooking for the rich and famous, the sooner you'll be able to film it all for your YouTube channel!'

'Seriously?' asked Dylan, his big blue eyes ready to jump out of his head. 'But you never let me film you cooking?'

'Well, If I end up cooking for someone famous I will! Not this Rock Star thing, not yet – but soon. I promise.'

'Mash my meatballs,' said Dylan. 'I've only got 36 subscribers on my channel. I'd kill to post something that goes viral!'

'So, what do you say?' asked Freddie. 'Fancy an adventure?'

Dylan gave a chocolatey smile. 'I'm in, as long as I can come with you. Mum heard his mansion is *gnizama!* Hey, do you think we'll get to meet Rock Rats?'

'Dunno,' said Freddie excitedly.

Dylan's mum's voice could be heard from their front room,

and she didn't sound happy.

'Uh-oh,' said Dylan, 'it's the fun police. I'm supposed to be tidying my room. Honestly, what do parents do all day while we're hard at work? Talk later, yeah?' Dylan headed for the hallway, stopping to turn and point at The Pockbury Times. 'And don't forget to *nib* the evidence!'

Freddie threw the newspaper in the bin and smiled, putting the last piece of KitKat in his mouth. He wondered in that moment if the delicious crispy wafer finger had ever tasted so good.

CHAPTER 4 - MUM

Freddie found his mum in the kitchen. Her long brown hair was tied in a ponytail, and she was covered in speckles of paint. She was trying to sing along to her favourite playlist, *'80's Rock'*, while admiring the half-painted New York skyline that was appearing on their kitchen wall.

His mum was always happiest when she was painting. She loved it so much that when she wasn't making artwork to sell online, she was working her way through the rooms of the house and painting the walls with different scenes. As she'd always dreamed of travelling the world, she wanted each room to make them feel like they'd been whisked away to another country. This way they could travel the world together without her having to leave the house.

Their front room was Freddie's favourite. He could sit on

their comfy sofa with a hot chocolate on a cold dreary day, and the walls would make him feel like he was on a beach under a palm tree in Jamaica. In their bathroom, he'd be on the loo in the middle of the Brazilian jungle, with snakes and spiders checking out his bottom. In his bedroom, he could swim with tropical fish along Australia's Great Barrier Reef without even having to hold his breath.

His mum had always encouraged her son to cook, and with good reason. She was an amazing artist, but a terrible cook. Give her a paint pot and she'd make something astonishing. Give her a cooking pot and she'd make something terrifying.

'Hi Freddie! Good day at school?'

'The usual,' said Freddie. 'Dylan got into trouble again with Mrs Straw.'

His mum laughed. 'I don't think I'd be too keen on being called *Mrs Warts* either!'

Freddie pointing at the wall. 'It's looking great, mum!'

'Thanks! So, what's on the menu tonight, chef? All this painting has made me hungry.'

'Alphabet lasagne with green bean Jenga,' said Freddie.

His mum laughed. 'Jenga? I spent years teaching you not to play with your food, and now you're asking me to play with *mine*! Dare I even ask what alphabet lasagne is?'

'ABC. Aubergines, beans and courgettes. We've got loads so I thought I'd experiment.'

'Perfect,' she replied, ruffling his scruffy brown hair.

'And what are those?' she asked, pointing to the tray on the kitchen worktop.

'Beetroot brownies. I'm experimenting with different types of cocoa to get the flavour right'.

His mum smiled. 'You do know when you're older I'll never want you to leave!'

Freddie carefully cut up the brownies and dusted them in icing sugar before placing them in an old Roses sweet tin. He washed his hands, then set off down the garden to his dad's veg patch. As a white butterfly danced around in front of him, he dropped to his knees, enjoying the feeling of the sun on his back. Freddie could picture his dad there whenever he wanted, and it brought him comfort. As he collected ingredients for tonight's creation from the rows of colourful leaves in front of him, he wondered what his dad would make of his crazy idea to cook for Rock Star.

His mum crossed the small patio. She threw a bag in the bin, then carried on down the garden and perched on the short wall next to Freddie.

'I miss him, mum.' He looked down at the beans and concentrated on them more than he needed to. He wiped away a small tear with the back of his hand and sniffed.

'I know you do. I miss him too. He'd be so proud of what you've done with his veg patch, he loved spending time out here with you. He loved cooking too; he'd be blown away by everything you've made!'

Freddie looked up at his mum. 'Do you think he's watching us right now?'

'I hope not,' she replied, tightening her scruffy brown ponytail, 'my hair's a right old mess! Oh, I don't know sweetheart. I like to think so. The one thing I do know is that if he could, he would. He'll also be checking to see if you've washed your hands properly, you could grow potatoes under those fingernails!'

'Is it ok if I make some soup in the morning?' asked Freddie, trying to sound as normal as possible.

'You mean *dishwasher juice*?' she replied, scrunching up her face. 'Why not. It's Saturday tomorrow, so I'll be having a nice lie in. Save some for your gran though, yeah? She's coming for tea.'

Freddie's mum shuffled off the wall and sat down next to Freddie on the edge of the grass. She put her arm round him and squeezed him tight until he almost lost his balance. They sat perfectly still for a few minutes, with neither of them wanting to move. She then gave that special 'hug noise' that people only ever use when they hug someone and pushed herself up off the grass. She bent down and kissed the top of his head before ruffling his scruffy brown hair and heading back in the direction of their perfect little home.

CHAPTER 5 - TV DINNERS

Freddie let himself into his best friend's house. He followed the familiar sounds and smells and found Dylan in the front room with his parents. The curtains were closed and all three of them were sitting in the dark with trays on their laps, watching the TV. As the only light was coming from the TV, it was hard to tell them apart. All three of them had wavy dark brown hair, and they were all the same round shape. Dylan's mum and dad even had small matching moustaches. If it wasn't for the fact that they were always in their favourite chairs, Freddie wouldn't have been able to tell which was which.

'Hi guys!' said Freddie, 'Can Dylan come and take Flash for a walk?'

Dylan's mum checked her watch and murmured something to her husband.

As Dylan's family had moved from Wales, his parents had a second language they could speak if they wanted to talk about Freddie but couldn't be bothered to get off the sofa. Over the years, Freddie had picked up a few words but hadn't told them. He'd just heard 'amser gwely' which meant bedtime, and 'cythruddo' which meant annoying. Freddie decided it was probably a good thing that he couldn't understand any more.

Dylan's mum replied without even taking her eyes off the telly. 'Back by 8 at the latest,' she said, with a mouthful of food. Freddie gave them his best forced smile and reversed out of the room with his friend.

The boys always took the same route when they took Flash for a walk. They turned right at the bottom of their road, walked down the main street, past the shops and right into Sid Shufflebottom park, aiming straight for their usual bench.

Freddie pulled a small parcel out of his back pocket and offered the contents to his friend.

'Are these what I think they are? *Seinworb?*'

Freddie nodded. 'Yep, brownies. They've got veg in, but don't let that put you off'.

'Cheers,' said Dylan, sniffing it before taking a large bite. 'Oh, mate! You've done it again!' Dylan licked his lips. 'You know, all the years we've been coming to this park, named after Rock Rats, and because of your cooking we finally might get the chance to meet him!'

'I know!' said Freddie, stroking Flash's black and white fluffy tail. 'Can you imagine if Rock Star actually eats something I've made?'

'As long as I don't have to eat it!' laughed Dylan. 'Not that you actually eat soup, it's more of a drink. And you shouldn't drink food, that's just weird.'

'Thanks for the encouragement, mate!' said Freddie. 'You're as bad as my mum calling it dishwasher juice!'

'But I love everything else,' Dylan added, 'especially your *ekac* and *eci maerc*!'

Freddie laughed. 'Tell you what, I'll make you an *ekac* as big as your head to say thanks. I know it's not the same as being able to film stuff for YouTube yet, but it's a start.'

'Cheers, mate!' said Dylan with a chocolatey smile. 'So, what time do you want me?'

Freddie thought for a moment. '8.30? Keep me company while I cook, then we can bike up to Rock Star's mansion when it's ready.'

'Whoah, you don't waste any time!' said Dylan.

'If I wait, I'll bottle it,' said Freddie, his nerves growing by the hour. 'I'm making him gran's favourite, my 'veg patch special'.'

'Are you going to tell your gran?' asked Dylan. 'She went to school with Rock Rats, didn't she?'

Freddie nodded. 'She did, yeah, but I don't think she knew him that well. No, let's keep this as our little secret.'

CHAPTER 6 - THE FIRST ATTEMPT

Freddie was a bag of nerves and excitement the following morning. Jumping out of bed, he opened his top drawer and smiled.

When Freddie had first started cooking, his gran had brought round a pile of his dad's old cookery books. They were by a famous chef called Keith Floyd. Confident, creative and crazy, he was everything Freddie wanted to be. As Keith Floyd wore a bow tie as well as an apron when he cooked, Freddie did the same. He liked to think of it as a cooking superhero costume. Every time we wore them, he dreamed he was cooking for someone rich and famous. And finally, this morning, he was.

For today's special cook, he knew exactly what he wanted to wear. His favourite bow tie in classic black that had originally belonged to his dad.

When Dylan came through the door, Freddie was staring at the fresh ingredients laid out in front of him on the kitchen worktop. He'd cooked this soup so many times he could have probably made it blindfolded but decided that might not be the brightest idea. Not wanting to take anything for granted today, he slowly chopped, blended, stirred and seasoned, tasting his creation every step of the way.

Dylan quietly watched his friend work as the delicious smell filled the air. He'd never seen Freddie concentrate so hard, treating the pan like it contained the most precious liquid in the world.

Finally, Freddie carefully poured the finished soup into his Dad's old tartan flask and screwed the lid on tight. He took his bow tie and apron off, laid them on the kitchen table and took a long deep breath. He stared at the flask, his heart feeling like it would beat right through his chest. 'Done!'

'You will be, if your mum finds out!' joked Dylan.

'Talking about my mum,' said Freddie, 'I've had an idea. If they ask, I'm going to say *mum* made the soup. That way it doesn't sound as weird. Mums are always making stuff for other people.'

'Not *your* mum,' said Dylan. 'She'd kill someone with her cooking!'

Freddie laughed. 'True! But she's not going to bump into him and tell him the truth, is she? Mum only ever goes to grans!'

'You can say it's one of those 'random acts of kindness' things your mum's always talking about,' Dylan replied. 'Old people love that!'

'Great idea,' said Freddie. He took one last look down the garden at his dad's old veg patch before picking up his helmet. 'Come on then, let's do this!'

They grabbed their bikes and set off down the road. The flask was hanging off Freddie's handlebar, banging into his left knee as he rode. They turned right onto the main road, past the row of shops, their school, and Sid Shufflebottom park. It was Saturday morning. Their small town was filled with noise, bustling with people and traffic heading one way or another on their own adventures.

Two miles out of Pockbury they found what they were looking for. To their right, a large wooden sign with big black letters read 'PRIVATE PROPERTY – KEEP OUT'. They pedalled slowly up the narrow tree-lined road. When they reached the top of the hill, the trees opened to reveal Rock Star's white mansion in the distance. They biked up the road until they came to an impressive set of tall gates. To their left was a small gatehouse. Freddie took his helmet off and noticed that the large metal gates in front of him looked like rows of guitars, and the fence railings had been designed to look like tall drumsticks. A large security guard was squeezing out of his gatehouse and walking quickly in their direction.

'Can I help you?' boomed the giant. The security guard was wider than Freddie was tall. His arms were so colossal that they didn't hang down like normal human arms. Instead, they stuck out sideways like ginormous chicken wings. Freddie's jaw dropped open.

'Lick a lamppost, he's huge!' whispered Dylan to his friend.

Freddie swallowed and took a few steps forward. 'Sorry to bother you, Sir, but my mum made this for your boss. It's homemade soup. She saw the article about Rock Star and wanted to help. She said it's a 'random act of kindness'.'

'Random act of kindness, eh? Step forward, boy,' bellowed the security guard, staring straight at Freddie.

Freddie gulped and shuffled forward a couple of small steps. He held the flask out in a hand that was shaking so much he didn't even recognise it as his own.

'What sort of soup is it?' the guard asked, currently blocking out the sun.

'Mum calls it *'veg patch special'*,' said Freddie, 'it's freshly made this morning with veg from our garden'.

Freddie noticed that the guard was so covered in tattoos that you couldn't imagine he'd ever been a child, let alone a cute baby. The tattoos ran from his fingers all the way up to the sides of his face. The boys both stood completely still, neither of them daring to move.

CHAPTER 7 - THE DELIVERY

The gentle voice that followed surprised them both.

'Isn't that thoughtful!' declared the guard. As a smile spread across his face all the way up to his eyes, he melted into something much more friendly.

'It's so sweet of you to help your mum too. Kids these days get such a bad reputation,' he continued, patting his huge hand on his chest.

The friends both breathed a sigh of relief. The guard took the flask from Freddie and carried it over to the gatehouse, saying something into his radio. The boys followed, unsure what to do.

The security guard turned and smiled. 'You've made my day, lads. Before Rock Star's accident there were parties every weekend. I used to be *so* busy with people coming and going.

Nowadays I sit in this tiny little hut all day long, nobody to talk to, bored out of my brain. I've even taken up knitting!' The guard held up a large knitting needle with a long multicoloured scarf hanging off it. Freddie smiled politely, hoping that Dylan wouldn't point out the obvious - that it was *definitely* more hole than scarf.

'It's not as exciting these days, but at least I don't have to lift anyone up by their ears anymore. My back's much better too,' he added with a smile, revealing a line of shiny gold teeth. He picked up a clipboard with his huge hands. 'Right then, matey - what's your mum's name and address?'

'My mum?' said Freddie, nervously glancing at Dylan. 'What do you need that for?'

The guard raised one eyebrow. 'You wouldn't believe the things that have been delivered here for Rock Star over the years. It's quietened down a lot these days, mind you. This'll get scanned, tested, the works – can't be too careful these days. So, name and address?'

Freddie gulped. 'It's Kate Wilson. 18 Hill Road, Pockbury.'

The guard scribbled the details down before looking directly at Freddie. 'And you are?'

'Me? Erm... I'm Freddie.'

The tap on the gates made the boys jump. They turned to see a man in gardening gloves resting on a pitchfork. He had dark hair and a friendly face. He was wearing the kind of trousers that were covered in a million pockets, and it looked like he had something sticking out of each one – a trowel, a roll of string and a tape measure were the most obvious. The guard handed the flask through the railings, and the man sprinted off in the direction of the house.

'Please say thanks to your mum for the soup, Freddie. That's made my day! Dave will get that checked and on its way up to the boss as soon as it's been given the 'all clear'. Cheers, boys!'

'Our pleasure!' replied Freddie, watching his Dad's special flask disappearing into the distance.

The guard turned sideways to squeeze back through the gatehouse door and waved goodbye. The friends grabbed their helmets and set off on their bikes the same way they came. Neither of them had ever felt so nervous, scared, and excited all at the same time. Their legs felt like jelly, but they were both beaming from ear to ear.

CHAPTER 8 - WHAT HAPPENS NEXT

They swung the bikes into their driveways as they always did, skidding to a stop on the gravel and turning to face each other.

'Fish my fingers! That was *looc*,' beamed Dylan.

'Can you believe the size of that security guard!' laughed Freddie.

'So, what happens next?'

'Dunno,' Freddie replied, 'I've got to get my dad's flask back somehow, so we've got a reason to go back!'

A bang on the window made Dylan jump. His mum was waving her arms in the air, and she didn't look happy.

'Fun police. Gotta go!'

Freddie squeezed down the side of the house, propped his bike up against the wall and locked their old rusty gate. It felt like a million miles away from the tall shiny gates he'd been stood in front of less than an hour ago. His mum was in the middle of adding the bright yellow taxi to the New York skyline on the kitchen wall and singing along to the radio.

She took a step back and studied her painting. 'Hi Freddie! Been anywhere nice?'

'Just down the park,' Freddie replied, scratching his nose so she couldn't spot the lie on his face.

'I've made you lunch. Don't worry, it's only a cheese sandwich - I haven't set fire to anything in your kitchen! Talking about food, what's on this evening's menu, chef?'

Freddie smiled. 'Chicken doughnuts with spinach crisps, then I'm making popping candy ice cream to go with the beetroot brownies.'

His mum laughed. 'Chicken doughnuts, eh? You are clever, I can't wait!'

Freddie stood next to his mum and looked at her latest artwork.

'The taxi's fab, mum.'

'Aww, thanks Freddie,' she replied. 'Painting's so much fun, especially when I've got some music to sing along to!'

Freddie cringed as his mum started singing along to the song playing in the background. 'Even if it is the wrong words, eh mum!'

'I don't know what you mean, son! *I'm* singing the right words, it's the *radio* that gets it wrong!' she replied with a wink. 'By the way, did you make your dishwasher juice... I mean, soup, this morning?'

'I certainly did,' said Freddie with a smile. 'Gran's favourite.' And hopefully someone else's favourite too, thought Freddie.

CHAPTER 9 - GRAN

Freddie's gran lived five minutes away in a small, pretty cottage – the kind you'd expect a gran to live in – but this was no average gran. While most grans had grey hair, Shirley's hair was bright pink. While most grans wore sensible shoes, Shirley wore Doc Martins. While most grans went to Bingo, Shirley *taught* Karate.

His gran loved Freddie's experimental dishes like prawn ice cream, sausage brownies and chocolate Yorkshire puddings. The only thing she had to be a little careful of were the chewier items because of her false teeth. Especially her top ones. Once you'd seen a family member fishing around a plate of food for their dentures, you couldn't unsee it.

As his gran walked into the kitchen, wearing a vintage Queen t-shirt and ripped jeans, Freddie ran straight over to her. He turned around with a smile and waited for the results of today's measuring session. She backed up to him and put her hand on top of their heads.

'I'm still winning,' she said, before turning and tickling him.

'I'm growing and you're shrinking, gran. It won't be long!'

She laughed. 'Cheeky!' Freddie's gran bent over groaning and pretended to be old and frail, before springing up and giving her grandson a playful karate chop on the arm. 'How's school?'

Freddie shrugged his shoulders. 'School's okay. Bit boring.'

'Boring?' his gran replied, 'Are you kidding me? There are 26 letters in the English alphabet, and if you put them in the right order, you have the most wonderful stories ever written. Same with maths, 10 simple little numbers and look at what we've achieved! We sent man to the moon using those tiny little digits. In my day…'

Freddie was saved by his mum walking into the kitchen. She gave their guest a big hug.

'Hi Shirley! Sorry to stop you in the middle of one of your 'in my day' speeches. Did you know Freddie made you some soup earlier?'

'Ooh, thanks Freddie, I'll make sure I take that home. It's always nice to give the 'old clackers' a rest!' she replied, snapping her teeth together with a wink before taking her usual seat at the table.

Freddie's mum joined her. 'Have you heard the news about your famous old schoolmate, Shirl? It's all over the news!'

'Oh Kate, I can't believe it! Someone told me about it at my Karate class earlier. That reporter Mark Dooley is a nasty piece of work, saying Sid 'hasn't got the guts for music anymore'. I can't believe Sid was daft enough to speak to him.'

Freddie's mum shook her head. 'Poor guy. You know I don't read that paper any more, but I switched the telly on earlier and it was on *every* channel.'

'It's gone viral!' added Freddie.

Freddie's gran rolled her eyes. '*Viral*? I don't understand why people say something's gone 'viral', it's not something you catch! The world's gone mad!'

Freddie opened his mouth to answer, but his gran was in one of her 'speech' moods.

'And another thing!' she added, 'Who gives that *plank* Mark Dooley the right to decide who's 'normal' these days? There are over 7 billion versions of normal on this planet. Doesn't he realise how much damage he can do with words?'

Freddie's mum shook her head. 'He doesn't care. Trust me, I should know! I just hope Rock Star's okay, bless him.'

His gran sighed. 'As do I. He's so young too, he's only 67.'

Freddie giggled and tried to turn it into a cough to disguise it.

'Just you wait, young man!' said his gran. 'You'll be 67 before you know it, then you'll have to put up with young people talking *sloooowly* to you like you're deaf, or stupid, or both. Honestly, kids these days!'

Freddie knew the next line that was coming, he'd heard it a million times before. He mouthed the words at the same time his gran said them.

'Old people aren't born old; we were young once too. We've all got stories to tell, if you take the time to listen.'

As Freddie dropped the chicken doughnuts into the fryer, he wondered how long it would be before he saw his dad's old flask again. He didn't have to wait long.

CHAPTER 10 - THE VISITOR

The knock on the door the next morning caught Freddie by surprise. He paused Keith Floyd halfway through stuffing a chicken and skipped to the front door. The man standing in front of him with a thick mop of dark hair looked strangely familiar. He recognised his dad's flask first, and the trousers with the million pockets second.

The man smiled and held out the flask. 'Hello, you must be Freddie? Sorry, I didn't get to introduce myself yesterday at the gatehouse. I'm Dave. I work for Rock Star.'

'Oh yeah, hi...' replied Freddie, taking the flask, and trying his best to smile back. Freddie hadn't expected anything to happen as quickly as this, and his mind was racing.

'Is your mum in? I wanted to have a quick word with her if I could.'

'No! Erm, she's gone out,' said Freddie.

Freddie knew exactly where his mum was, and it wasn't out. She was upstairs in the bath. Fortunately for Freddie, his mum took ridiculously long baths. She'd light candles, listen to music through her headphones and spend at least an hour in there until she was as wrinkled as a raisin. By Freddie's calculations, that gave him at least 45 minutes before *splashdown*.

Dave checked his watch. 'I can come back later if that's any better?'

'Not really, she's *very* shy,' Freddie replied.

'Oh, okay. Can I leave her a message?' asked Dave, patting down his million pockets. 'I don't suppose you've got a pen? Turns out it's the only thing I haven't brought!'

'Sure,' replied Freddie. He turned to go down the hallway and stopped. He didn't want Dave to meet his mum, but he also didn't want to be rude. He decided to take a risk.

'Come in,' said Freddie, 'I'm sure there's one in the kitchen.'

Dave followed him down the hall. Freddie found a pen next to his pile of Keith Floyd cookery books. When he turned round, Dave was standing in the doorway checking out the garden.

'Great veg patch. Is that your dads?' asked Dave.

'It was. It's mine now.'

'Mind if I look? I'm a keen gardener myself. Once you've eaten home grown veg, all that supermarket stuff seems tasteless. I'd have loved something like this when I was your age.'

Freddie followed Dave out into the garden. 'Why didn't you?'

'I never had the chance! I grew up in the middle of a city, nobody had a garden where I lived. Then I left school and toured with the band. When the boss moved back home, he offered me a job as a handyman. Best thing I ever did. Now I've got my own little garden up there with my own veg patch, and I absolutely love it.'

Freddie looked surprised. '*You* were in the band?'

Dave laughed. 'Me? I'm not *that* old, I'm only 36! Rock Star's old enough to be my dad! No, I used to carry all their equipment. Crikey, I need a shave if I'm looking that rough!'

Dave walked over to the strawberry plants, knelt beside them and carefully inspected the leaves.

Freddie sighed. 'I know, they're a right old mess. I keep spraying this stuff on them that's supposed to put the birds off, but it's not working.'

'You know what you need?' said Dave, squinting in the sun. 'A net. Pop a net over the strawberries and that'll sort it.' He brushed the dirt off his trousers as he stood up. 'Right, about this soup. The boss absolutely loved it. I don't suppose your mum would be interested in coming up to meet him? I think he's keen on paying her to make this a regular thing.'

Freddie quickly jumped up off the ground. 'What? No way!'

Dave smiled. 'Tell you what, instead of leaving her a note, can you give her a quick call and ask her what she thinks?'

CHAPTER 11 - THE 'MUM' CALL

Freddie's mind was racing. 'Erm, sure! I'll find my phone. One sec!'

He ran inside and found his phone on the sofa in the front room. He called Dylan, gave his friend the thirty second version and carefully listened to the reply.

'Are you sure?' asked Freddie, worried his friend had lost the plot. He ended the call, changed Dylan's name in his phone to 'Mum', and quickly called his friend back. He then ran back outside, pointing at the screen and passing the phone to Dave as instructed. 'Mum wants to speak to you.'

Dave looked at the phone before putting it to his ear. 'Hello?'

Dylan squeaked in his best 'mum' voice. 'Oh, yes, hello Dave! I'm Freddie's mum – but you can call me Kate.' Dylan paused to hide a giggle. 'I believe your boss is considering placing an order for my delicious soup on a regular basis?'

Dave looked a little baffled. 'Err, hi Kate... yeah, that's right!'

Dylan was watching Freddie and Dave in the garden from his bedroom window and trying not to laugh. 'I'm happy to do that, but you would need to deal with my son. He's my manager, you know.' Dylan covered the handset and giggled.

Dave scratched his head. 'Really?'

Dylan composed himself before continuing in his high-pitched voice. 'Oh, absolutely! I'm so *terribly* shy you see. It's that or nothing I'm afraid!'

Dave turned to Freddie and smiled. 'Okay, well thanks Kate, I'll speak to your... manager, I suppose? Bye!'

Freddie looked over Dave's shoulder at his best friend's bedroom window. He could see Dylan laughing and pulling funny faces.

Dave looked at the phone again before handing it back. 'Wow, she must be shy!'

'Like you wouldn't believe!' replied Freddie, hoping his limited drama skills were working.

'Looks like you'll be coming up to meet the boss then!' said Dave. 'Shall we say next Saturday? About 11ish? If there's any chance your mum can make some more of that soup by then, even better.'

'Sure!' said Freddie, pausing for a second. 'One more thing. Can I bring a friend?'

CHAPTER 12 - STAR'S BAR

The best friends were bursting with excitement when they arrived at the gatehouse on Saturday morning. Neither of them could believe they were about to meet one of the most famous musicians in the world.

The huge, tattooed security guard put down his knitting and gave Freddie and Dylan a big smile, his gold teeth sparkling in the sunshine. The voice that followed was as gentle as they remembered, and still as much of a surprise.

'Hello again, boys! I'll let Dave know you've arrived.' The guard pressed a button before squeezing sideways out of the gatehouse door. 'I hear your mum's homemade soup went down a storm. They say the way to a man's heart is through his stomach. Bit tricky when he doesn't have one!' The guard put his hands on his hips and laughed at his own joke. 'Ah, here's

Dave now. I'll leave you in his capable hands.'

'Thanks, Mr. Security Guard,' beamed Freddie.

'Please, it's Tom – or you can call me what the boss does - Tiny Tom!'

Dylan laughed loudly and shook his hand. 'Hi Tiny Tom, I'm Dylan.'

Tiny Tom turned to Freddie, smiled and held out his huge hand. Freddie shook it before turning to see what the unusual sound was. Dave pulled up to the gatehouse in what looked like a golf buggy. The trousers with the million pockets had gone, replaced with a t-shirt, tracksuit bottoms and trainers.

'Hello again Freddie,' said Dave with a smile, jumping off and introducing himself to Dylan. 'Hop on lads, and I'll take you up to meet the boss. Hold on tight, this thing *really* motors!'

The boys jumped on the back and gripped onto the bar in front of them with both hands. Freddie put the flask between his knees and held on tight. The buggy set off with a jump before crawling along the road. They could have walked faster. Freddie turned to Dylan who was still gripping the bar and laughed. The grounds reached as far as the eye could see. As they slowly approached the mansion, the huge water fountain in the middle of the driveway caught their attention. The statue in the centre of the fountain was of Rock Star playing a guitar. Water was shooting out of the guitar head as the figure steadily spun around.

Dylan leaned over to his friend. 'Squeeze my spots, this place is *evissam*!'

Freddie looked up at the mansion that towered above him and swallowed, trying to keep his breakfast in his stomach. They came to a stop in front of the mansion. Dave jumped off the buggy and the boys followed him up the white stone steps. The pillars at either side of the door made it feel like they were about to walk into Buckingham Palace. Right now, Freddie didn't know who would be the scariest to meet – the king of rock, or the King of England.

They nervously stepped through the vast double doors and into a hall that was bigger than both of their houses put together. It had grand staircases leading from the left and the right. The walls on both sides were covered with photos of a young Rock Star and a whole list of celebrities. The hair on most of them was bigger than their actual heads, long and curly, like they'd all been to the same hairdresser. They reminded Freddie of a dog his Grandma used to have.

Dave pointed to the room on the left. 'Make yourself at home and I'll let the boss know you're here. Cheryl will look after you.'

The best friends stood in the doorway of the room with their mouths wide open. It certainly wasn't what they'd been expecting. It was like stepping into a real-life pub, but in someone's house. The sign above the door said, 'Star's Bar'. There was a pool table in the middle of the room and a dartboard on the wall to their left. Along the wall to their right was a line of old arcade machines, all flashing and making noises. At the back of the room was a long bar with a row of stools in front of it. Behind the bar was a woman who they suspected must be Cheryl. She had long blonde hair, and she was wearing a black apron with 'Star's Bar' on the front. Polishing a glass and holding it up to the light to inspect it, she looked over in their direction and gave them a smile.

High above their heads a disco ball was spinning slowly, reflecting shiny little squares that danced on the ceiling. The walls were covered in old musical instruments (some with bite marks and some without) and lots of huge, signed movie posters. Freddie looked down at the rows of black circles on the floor. He'd seen some of these circles in the loft once. They were old music records, the kind his Dad used to listen to.

The voice behind them made the boys jump.

'*Vinyl* flooring! Get it? Made with real vinyl records. I gave my designer a list of all the records that had ever been above me in the charts and we bought the lot. Now they're under me and I can walk all over them! Makes me smile every day. Hi, boys! I'm Rock Star...'

CHAPTER 13 - FIRST IMPRESSIONS

Rock Star wasn't at all what the boys were expecting. The old man that stood before them in a tracksuit and slippers was completely bald and nearly the same height as them. On the TV, with his big curly black hair, make-up and leather trousers, he looked about seven feet tall.

'So, which one of you is Freddie?' asked Rock Star, looking from one boy to the other.

Freddie nervously held up his hand.

'Hi Freddie, nice to meet you. There's no reason to be shy, I promise I don't bite. Well, not these days!'

Freddie tried to smile.

'I used to know another Freddie. Freddie Mercury. Mad as a box of frogs, but I loved him to bits.'

Freddie's eyes lit up. 'That's who I'm named after!'

'No way!' exclaimed Rock Star. 'Your oldies have got great taste, man! I played guitar with Freddie and his band Queen when I first started out. He's a legend!'

Rock Star turned from one boy to the other. 'And who do we have here then?'

Dylan looked he was going to explode with excitement.

'Hi *Rock Rats*, I'm Dylan!'

As soon as the words came out of Dylan's mouth he froze. He looked at Freddie and cringed.

'Sorry!' Dylan blurted, 'I have this thing with words...'

Rock star laughed and waved his hand. 'Rock Rats, eh? I love it! Trust me, I've been called much worse! *Dylan*, you say? I knew one of those, too. I toured America with Bob Dylan back in the 80's. We went on a 24-hour sun chasing party in my private jet. Man, that was wild!'

Freddie struggled to imagine that the man in front of them could get on an airplane, let alone travelling around America, but he remembered what his gran said. 'Old people aren't born old; they were young once too. They've all got stories to tell, if you take the time to listen.'

As Rock Star shuffled over to the bar, Freddie opened his mouth. 'If you don't mind me saying, you look a bit different to what we expected?'

Rock Star perched on a stool and beckoned for them to join him.

'I'll let you into a secret, lads.'

CHAPTER 14 – CURLY WIGS

Freddie and Dylan edged closer.

'To be honest, I don't even recognise myself. These last few months have made me realise that it's *much* more comfortable to act my age. Those tight leather trousers were a *nightmare*! They'd take ages to get on and they were horribly sweaty. Same with that big bushy wig – it was incredibly itchy, but I didn't want my fans to know how *bald* I was getting. I'm pleased to see the back of those gold medallions too. They were so heavy I couldn't even stand up straight. Tracksuits, man - they're so comfy!'

Freddie couldn't help but giggle.

'Getting ready every morning used to be such a tough gig. It took me over an hour to untangle my curly wig and do my eye make-up, now I'm washed and dressed in three minutes flat.

These days I can chill out and watch home renovation programmes all morning in complete comfort. I don't even have to worry any more about getting eye liner on the cushions. Did I mention the slippers? Oh, man! They're a revelation - my feet have never been so toasty! And pockets - don't even get me started on pockets. So practical!'

Rock put his hand on his stomach and sighed. 'What I *do* miss is proper food, especially stinky cheese. Having no stomach is like having a tube that runs from one set of cheeks to the other. The doctors also told me I'm now lactose intolerant, which means I can't eat any *dairy* products either. Cheese, ice creams, milkshakes, they've all had to go. It's hard enough not being able to eat another guitar, but cheese? I'd sell all my cars if I could eat stinky cheese again!'

Dylan couldn't help but feel sorry for him. 'Dunk my doughnuts, that sucks.'

'Tell me about it,' said Rock Star. 'I tried the tiniest bite, and it was more painful than listening to the radio! Chart music these days, lads - it's all noise! All that talking instead of singing, and everyone sounds so flippin' miserable. Honestly,

I've heard better sounds coming from my toilet!'

Rock Star let out a long sigh. 'Sorry lads, listen to me going on! Right, enough of that. Cheryl, my usual please. Water on the rocks! What's your tipple, boys? Whisky? Lager? Hang on, I've got it. Cheryl, get these boys a vodka and orange... without the vodka!'

The conversation flowed so much easier than the boys could have ever dreamed of. They talked about their school and how much it had changed since Rock Star had been a pupil there over 50 years ago. They asked the rocker about the places he'd been and the people he'd met, and they listened so hard they lost all track of time.

Rock Star suddenly pointed at the pool table. 'Hey, I don't suppose either of you play?'

'*Yletulosba!*' exclaimed Dylan.

Rock Star looked confused.

'He's Welsh,' said Freddie, hoping that would explain Dylan's strange way with words. 'He means *absolutely*. We'd love a game!'

'We used to play pool at youth club,' added Dylan, 'until

someone stole two of the table legs.'

'Well then, lads,' chuckled Rock Star, 'what are we waiting for?'

He passed the boys two pool cues before carefully choosing his own.

'In fact, I've had an idea. As I've been told you're the one to talk to about your mum's soup, how about we make this game more interesting?'

'Okay?' Freddie replied, looking confused.

'How about this? The winner sets the price for a large flask of soup to be delivered here every week. Do we have a deal?'

CHAPTER 15 - THE POOL GAME

'Deal!' said Freddie excitedly.

'Excellent!' replied Rock Star. 'Let's get some music on then, shall we? Freddie, this one's for you.'

Rock Star walked over to the jukebox, pressed a few keys and waited for the song to start. Freddie recognised it straight away, he'd been named after the singer. It was 'Don't Stop Me Now' by Queen, one of his gran's favourites.

Rock Star gestured for the boys to break. Freddie took a deep breath, chalked his cue and composed himself. He launched the cue ball straight into the pack. The yellow and red balls scattered all over the table, but surprisingly nothing dropped down into the pockets.

Rock Star danced over to the table, holding his pool cue like a guitar and pretending to play.

'My turn!'

He bent down and took his shot. Three balls dropped into pockets – two red and one yellow.

'I'll be reds, boys!' said Rock Star, quickly pocketing another red. 'I've missed playing pool these last few months. This place used to be *packed* with people coming and going, and now it's as empty as my insides!' As Rock Star pocketed yet another tricky red, Freddie looked over at Dylan in disbelief. This wasn't looking good.

'Tiny Tom's a great security guard,' said Rock Star, 'but he can't play pool for toffee. His arms are so big he can't hold the pool cue properly, he misses the balls and rips the cue right through the cloth. I've had it replaced more times than I've had hot dinners. Well, this year at least!'

Freddie and Dylan watched helplessly as Rock Star pocketed another red ball before finally missing a shot. Dylan stepped forward and chose his target. A simple enough yellow, hanging directly over the pocket. He hit the cue ball perfectly, but instead of the yellow ball dropping into the pocket it wobbled around in the jaws before popping back out again.

'That's strange,' mumbled Freddie.

Rock Star bent down and pocketed yet another ball. 'Last red, boys!' he declared, hitting what looked like an impossible shot only for the red to land directly in the middle of the pocket. Before the boys could speak, Rock Star potted the black and held the pool cue in the air.

'I win!'

Freddie scratched his head. Staring at the table in astonishment, he noticed something very odd. The pocket nearest to him was slowly shrinking. He looked over at Rock Star, who was lifting his thumb off a small button at the end of his cue.

'Cheat!' shouted Freddie, covering his mouth as he remembered who he was speaking to.

Rock Star looked directly at him, holding his hand to his chest and trying his best to look offended. The expression slowly changed to a smile, and he held his hands up. 'Okay, you got me. I hadn't played in ages, so I thought I might need a little help. My designer had this pocket gizmo fitted to the table. I can make the pockets bigger or smaller with the press of a button on my cue. You must admit, it's pretty cool!'

'It's *totally* cool, Rock Rats,' said Dylan, 'but it's still cheating.'

Rock Star sighed. 'I know, I'm sorry. Maybe that reporter Mark Dooley's right, maybe I haven't 'got the guts' to play *anything* anymore.' He walked over to the bar, picked up a white cloth and waved it in the air. 'Okay, I surrender. You win. Freddie, name your price.'

Freddie gestured for his friend to join him in the corner of the room, and they whispered to each other for a minute. Finally, Freddie took a deep breath and turned to face Rock Star. 'I was going to say £20, but I've had an idea. £15 a week for a flask of homemade soup *and* we get to give you a game of pool.'

Rock Star walked to the bar, poured himself another glass of water, and sat on a stool. He thought for a moment and then shook his head. 'I'm sorry, Freddie. I can't accept that...'

CHAPTER 16 - THE DEAL

Freddie looked down at his feet. He knew he'd pushed his luck.

Rock Star continued '...it's nowhere near enough! £100 a week, *and* a game of pool. That's my final offer.'

Freddie looked at Dylan, whose mouth had dropped open.

'£100?' asked Freddie, in shock. 'Are you serious?'

Rock Star laughed. 'I haven't been this serious since I signed my first record contract! That soup of your mums is worth every penny.'

Freddie smiled from ear to ear. 'Wow! Thanks, Rock Star. It's a deal!'

Dylan squealed and punched the air.

Rock Star gave Freddie a firm handshake. 'Brilliant! That soup is the first thing I've *enjoyed* eating in months. The only thing that could make it any better would be if it tasted of stinky cheese!'

Rock Star rubbed his chin, paused, and then pointed at Freddie. 'In fact, I have a challenge. Tell your mum if she can make me a soup that tastes of stinky cheese, without actually *containing* stinky cheese, I'll double it. I don't care what she puts in it – trust me when I say I've eaten a *lot* of weird and wonderful things over the years – there's only one rule. Absolutely no dairy. Agreed?'

'Agreed!' exclaimed Freddie, hardly able to contain his excitement.

They played another game of pool, this time for fun. As Freddie watched Rock Star walking round the pool table, he couldn't help but think about the hurtful things that Mark Dooley had said about him in the newspaper.

'Rock Star?' said Freddie, 'It's probably not my place to say anything - I mean, what do I know, I'm a kid, right? But one thing I do know is that Mark Dooley says horrible things about everyone. You're not the only one.'

'Really?' asked Rock Star.

'Oh yeah!' added Dylan, 'you should ask my mum! She came

second in his list of *Pockbury's Ugliest Residents* last month.'

'No way!' said an astonished Rock Star. 'Was she upset?'

'Upset? She was fuming! Mum loves a trophy. She was hoping for first place, she'd been growing her moustache especially!'

Rock Star looked like he didn't know whether to laugh or apologise.

'The point is,' added Freddie, quickly changing the subject, 'he's always writing nasty stuff. Mum used to work there, and she left because he was so horrible to her. My gran says Mark Dooley's a plank.'

'Does she now?' Rock Star replied. 'It sounds like your gran's right! Thanks Freddie, that means a lot. I'm sorry to hear about your mum too. If Mark Dooley doesn't want her, I certainly do. Get back home and tell your mum to start cooking. For the first time in months, I can't wait for next weekend!'

He wasn't the only one.

CHAPTER 17 - THE CHALLENGE

It had been three days since they'd met Rock Star and still Freddie couldn't sleep. Staring at the cobweb in the corner on his bedroom ceiling, he desperately searched every corner of his mind for ideas. He was over the moon that Rock Star liked his soup, but now he'd met the man, he wanted to help even more.

School was a bit of a blur. He sat at his desk quietly repeating the words under his breath. 'Like stinky cheese, no dairy, anything goes.' As soon as Freddie got home, he grabbed an armful of cookery books and sat down at the table. He was lost in his own little world when his mum walked into the kitchen. She was wearing her painting clothes and had speckles of paint on her fingers.

'Hi sweetheart! Homework first, you know the rules.'

'This *is* homework,' lied Freddie, his head lost in a book.

Freddie's mum put her hands on her hips. 'Oh yes, tell me more?'

Playing for time, Freddie picked up the glass in front of him. He drank slowly while racking his brain for something *mum-proof*. 'My new food tech teacher has set us a challenge, and he wants it in by Saturday.' As soon as the words had left his mouth, he knew he'd made a mistake. She folded her arms.

'But you don't go to school on a Saturday?'

'Oh, err, well obviously I know *that*,' he replied, taking an even slower drink. 'My teacher's in school, though. We get extra points if we drop our food in by lunchtime.'

Freddie hid his face behind the cookery book. His mum had always possessed a special power for knowing if he was telling the truth or not. He often thought that when a person was being asked if they committed a crime, they didn't need a jury to guess whether a stranger is telling the truth. It should be their mum, with her arms folded and a disappointed look on her face. It would be better than any lie detector test.

His mum started smiling. 'A free lunch, eh? I like his style!

Right, I've got some painting to do. Give me a shout if you need me!'

'Sure,' replied Freddie. He walked down to his dad's veg patch with the cookery books under his arm. As he flicked through the pages, Dylan squeezed through the loose fence panel. 'How's it going?'

'Don't ask,' replied Freddie. 'I've searched online and can't find a thing. Dad's books were my last hope!' Freddie paced up and down the garden, muttering the words 'like stinky cheese, no dairy, anything goes' repeatedly.

Before long, Dylan threw his arms in the air. 'Mate, put a sock in it, you're doing my head in! If I hear that one more time I'm going to scream!'

Freddie turned to look at his friend. 'What did you say?'

'I said I'm going to scream!' repeated Dylan.

'No, no, before that...'

Dylan looked confused. 'Put a sock in it?'

'Mate, that's it!' squealed Freddie, racing through the kitchen door.

CHAPTER 18 - THE SOLUTION

Freddie raced upstairs and into the bathroom. He found his mum's special box in its usual place, between the python and the tarantula that were painted on the bathroom wall. For the first time ever, the sight of it made him smile.

Freddie's mum's feet had always been on the smelly side, but in the last couple of years they were off-the-charts dangerous. On a hot day, Freddie could track his mum down by following the wet footprints on the floor. He always tried his hardest not to say anything, but holding his breath through a whole episode of MasterChef in their front room was impossible. Freddie would sit there wishing that the tropical scene his mum had painted on the wall was scratch and sniff, so that he could enjoy the gentle fragrance of palm trees and sea air instead of something that smelled like a dead hamster wrapped in cheese.

To keep the problem under control, Freddie's mum kept her smelly socks in a special box. When her feet became so sweaty that her socks started to squelch, she would throw them into the box and immediately lock it down. When the box was full, she would tip the socks into a big pan of water and boil them to get the smell out. And now, that's exactly what Freddie planned to do – but for very different reasons.

With his mum's special box sloshing under his arm, he rejoined his friend in the garden.

'Dylan, you're a genius! 'Put a sock in it' - that's the solution! Like stinky cheese, no dairy, anything goes!'

Dylan stared at the box in disbelief. 'Mate, it's an expression! You can't use your mum's socks - they *knits*!'

'Exactly! Mum's socks are the stinkiest and cheesiest things in the world!' Freddie carefully lifted the lid off the box and sniffed the air. The smell was so strong it felt like his nose hairs were on fire. 'The missing ingredient has been right here under my nose this whole time, and there's a never-ending supply!'

Dylan looked at his friend in disbelief. 'Mate, are you

seriously forgetting what happened last year? When Mark Dooley fired her and put your mum on the front page of the newspaper? 'The Smelliest Feet in Town Award', remember?'

'Of course I remember!' snapped Freddie. 'Gran and I were the ones that had to pick up the pieces. Mum cried for weeks she was so embarrassed. She couldn't go anywhere without someone pointing and laughing, that's why she stopped going out. The stress made her feet smell even worse.'

'Yep,' shuddered Dylan, 'dad made us keep our windows closed for weeks. And you really want to go back there? To the dressing gown days?'

Freddie shook his head. 'Course not, but think about it! She ended up dusting off all her old art stuff and painting again, and now she's a *proper artist*! She set up that website too, *Soul Mates*, to help people with the same problem. She's always talking to people on there, and she's made loads of friends. I know mum doesn't go out much still, but you can tell she's happy cos she's singing again.'

'If you can call it singing,' said Dylan.

'And think of the bigger picture! With the money Rock Star's talking about, I could properly be the man of the house! This could be *life changing!*'

Dylan shuddered and lifted up the special box, watching the sweaty liquid running from side to side as he moved it. 'Or *life taking*! Mate, I've got a bad feeling about this. I know your mum calls soup dishwasher juice - well this would be... *sock juice*! I mean, what's even in this stuff? I know Rock Rats thinks he's indestructible, but you can't give him something that might actually poison him!'

Freddie paused for a second. 'Okay. Here's the deal. I'll check online to see what sweat is made of, but if there's nothing in there that's dangerous, I'm doing it. I mean, what's the worst that could happen?'

CHAPTER 19 - THE SCIENCE LESSON

They sat in the garden while Freddie clicked and scrolled on his phone. Dylan spent the next few minutes shaking his head, eating one of Freddie's homemade chocolate cookies and playing with Flash. Suddenly, Freddie looked up with a cheeky smile.

'Looks like I've found myself a new ingredient!'

'Really?' asked Dylan, cringing. 'What does it say?'

Freddie took a deep breath and sat up straight. 'So, our bodies contain different kinds of bacteria, yeah?'

Dylan pulled a face. 'Go on...'

'They're tiny little creatures that live on our skin. When our feet get warm and start sweating, the bacteria go crazy for the salt in the sweat, and they start munching on it. The bacteria make a stinky waste, and that's where the smell comes from.'

Dylan puffed his cheeks out. 'Grim! So why does it smell like cheese?'

'This bit's *really* cool,' announced Freddie, resting back on the grass. 'Certain stinky cheeses have exactly the same bacteria growing on the outside as we do. Same bacteria, same stinky waste, same stinky smell!'

'Let me make sure I've got this right,' said Dylan. 'You're basically telling me that stinky cheese is covered in bacteria poo? And those same bacteria are currently having a mega-party on your mum's feet?'

Freddie laughed. 'You *could* put it like that! They're like a team of tiny workers, and they get paid in sweat.'

'Eww! And what's sweat made of?' asked Dylan cautiously.

'99% of sweat is water,' said Freddie.

'Really? Wow, that last one percent has got to be made of some scary stuff!'

'Chemicals,' replied Freddie, 'ammonia, urea, salts and sugar.'

'Sugar!' replied Dylan. 'At last, a word I like!'

Freddie chuckled. 'Anyway, as long as you don't drink a

whole pint of sweat on its own, it's fine.'

Dylan's imagination ran wild for a minute, and the colour drained from his cheeks.

'Okay Freddie, next question. If Rock Rats is going to start paying you megabucks, what are you going to do with all this money?'

'I think I've come up with a plan for that,' said Freddie. 'You know her Soul Mates website?'

Dylan nodded. 'Her smelly feet mates, yeah?'

'That's the one! Mum's met loads of people through it, she helps them by sharing tips and stuff. Someone in America asked to pay for her help, so mum set up this 'buy me a coffee' thing. People can click a link and send money, and they don't even have to leave their name. I could give Rock Star that link! Mum will get the money and she'll think it's someone she's helped on her website. What do you reckon?'

'Sounds like a plan,' said Dylan, 'but is there any chance I can have something too?'

Freddie folded his arms. 'As well as the chocolate cake and the chance to hang out with Rock Star every weekend?'

'Let me film you cooking?' pleaded Dylan. 'I promise I won't post it on my YouTube page or anything. I only want the practice for when I've hit the big time. Pleeeease?'

'Okay, it's a deal!' said Freddie.

'Ride a rhinoceros!' exclaimed Dylan, punching the air. 'So, when can I film you making this new 'death by sock juice' thing?'

Freddie thought for a second. 'Friday? We're supposed to be going to grans. I'll tell mum I'm not feeling well and make it while she's out.'

'Hey, do the beans-in-the-toilet thing, that one always works!' said Dylan excitedly. 'Boil my brains, I can't believe I'm finally going to film you cooking! This is going to be *emosewa*!'

'What?' asked a very confused Freddie.

Dylan gave Freddie a big chocolatey smile.

'Awesome!'

CHAPTER 20 - THE FIRST ATTEMPT

It was Friday evening. Freddie heard the familiar creak of his mum coming up the stairs. He opened the can of beans and waited for the tap on the bathroom door.

'Sweetheart, are you feeling any better?'

Freddie held the can of beans high above the toilet and tipped some out.

'Splosh!' Freddie prepared his best poorly voice. 'Not really, mum. I think I need to stay here.' He tipped the rest of the beans into toilet. 'SPLOSH!'

Freddie's mum pulled a face.

'You don't sound too good. I'll give your gran a call...'

'No, no, no,' cried Freddie, 'there's no point both of us missing out. I'll text you if I need you.'

'Are you sure? I honestly don't mind staying...'

'Please go, mum. I promise I'll be fine,' said Freddie, stifling a giggle.

The front door closed. Freddie guessed he had about three hours before his mum would be walking back through the front door. That should give him enough time. He went to his room, opened his drawer and quickly picked out the bow tie and apron most suitable for the job. His favourite, classic black. They'd already proved to be lucky as he'd worn them when he made his first soup for Rock Star. He crossed his fingers and hoped they were going to be lucky again.

He grabbed his mum's special box from the bathroom and carefully carried it downstairs. Looking across at the cover of his favourite cookbook, Freddie wondered what Keith Floyd would make of him using his mum's smelly socks as an ingredient. Freddie turned to find Flash staring up at him. Did Flash know what he was up to? A flush of red appeared on Freddie's guilty cheeks.

Dylan walked through the back door. 'How's it going?'

'Like clockwork,' replied Freddie. 'Those beans worked a treat; she thought I was properly sick!'

Dylan laughed. 'I told you! Mum falls for it every time!' Dylan looked over at the special box and shuddered. 'Mate, last chance. Are you sure you want to do this?'

'Where's your sense of adventure?' asked Freddie. 'You know, many years ago, someone watched an *egg* fall out the back end of a chicken and was brave enough to pick it up and eat it!'

'There's a fine line between brave and stupid,' muttered Dylan, setting up his phone.

Freddie swiftly gathered the ingredients he needed from the veg patch and raced back to the kitchen. He washed, chopped and diced faster than he ever had before. With onions, carrots, tomatoes, celery and herbs flying all over the chopping board, he shared the ingredients between two pans. One for Rock Star's normal soup, and one for the *experimental* batch. Dylan filmed from the door as Freddie chopped, poured and stirred.

Finally, it was time for the star ingredient. Freddie switched on the extractor fan while Dylan stepped back towards the open door. Wincing a little, Freddie carefully opened his mum's special box.

'Here we go!' said Freddie, lifting a single sock out of the box with tongs before lowering it into the unsuspecting pan. 'Mum's non-dairy-cheesy-flavour-bomb!' He quickly closed the box, put the lid back on the pan and ran to the doorway for some fresh air.

'It's definitely a bomb alright, your mum's socks are like lethal weapons! How long will it take?' asked Dylan, checking the recording on his phone.

'The longer I give it, the stronger it'll be. I'll try 45 minutes,' said Freddie, setting the timer.

The boys filled the time by playing football, dribbling the ball to each other when Flash would let them. When the oven timer buzzed, Freddie ran straight in through the open back door. Dylan followed closely behind him, phone back in hand, keeping a sensible distance away from the experimental cooking.

Dylan lifted his phone and pressed record.

CHAPTER 21 - THE RESULTS ARE IN

Freddie sniffed it before turning to look at his friend. He grabbed a large wooden spoon and held it to his chin like a microphone, much to Dylan's amusement.

'Ladies and gentlemen, thank you for joining us for this year's MasterChef final. You've joined us at a crucial moment in the competition. This experimental *sock juice* certainly smells like super stinky cheese, but how does it taste?'

Aware that at any minute the smell might overpower him, he carefully spooned some of the liquid into a small white bowl before walking over to the kitchen table. Dylan inched closer.

Freddie inspected the soup like it was the most interesting dish he'd ever laid eyes on. He pushed the watery contents around with the spoon before bravely lifting some to his mouth. He blew gently, steadied himself, then slurped the tiniest amount in through his lips. Dylan zoomed in and watched carefully, holding his breath and waiting for some kind of reaction. Freddie closed his eyes, moved the spoon back to his lips, and slurped up the remainder of the soup. As he opened his eyes a small smile appeared, followed by the biggest grin his face was capable of.

'No way!' said Dylan, still recording.

'The results are in!' announced Freddie. 'The winner of this year's MasterChef final is... me!'

Dylan started giggling. 'Pop my Pringles, that's *deckiw* - but still totally gross! And you're really sure we're not going to kill Rock Rats?'

'Are you kidding me?' Freddie replied. 'This guy has eaten guitars, drumsticks, microphones... everything! Rock Star drinking sock juice would be like *us* drinking orange juice. The main thing is we're sticking to the rules. Does it smell like stinky cheese? *Definitely.* Is it dairy free? *Completely.* Is it anything goes? *Absolutely!*'

'True,' said Dylan, laying his phone down, 'but I think we should keep the whole *sock* thing a secret ingredient for now.

After all, if Rock Rats really likes the stuff and you tell him what's in it, he might get some fancy chef to make it for him. Then you're out of a job. It needs a name too; we can't keep calling it *sock juice!*'

Freddie nodded. 'Good point! Any ideas?'

'Leave it with me,' replied Dylan, 'I'll come up with something. Oh, and Freddie?'

'Yeah?' said Freddie, studying the bowl with a huge grin on his face.

'That's definitely one bowl I don't want to lick! Right, catch you later!' Dylan headed back down the garden and disappeared through the broken fence panel.

Freddie filled Rock Star's large flask with the vegetable soup. Grabbing his dad's old tartan flask, he carefully poured in his new creation. He added his mum's sock back into her special box before carrying out the final part of his plan.

He messaged his mum telling her that he was feeling better, and that he'd even managed to make the soup for his so-called 'food tech challenge'. Not only did that cover his tracks, but it also meant he had the perfect excuse to go out and deliver his latest invention to Rock Star's mansion. After all, the last thing he needed was his mum telling him he had to stay in bed when he had an important business meeting with an international superstar.

CHAPTER 22 - THE SECOND VISIT

Freddie was waiting outside on his bike at 10am sharp. As he didn't fancy having both his knees banged by flasks hanging off his handlebars all the way to Rock Star's mansion, this time he was wearing his trusty rucksack.

Dylan appeared with his bike in one hand and a cereal bar in the other. He looked up at the sun and squinted. 'Perfect weather for hanging out with a rock legend!'

'Even better if he likes my new soup,' said Freddie quietly, looking over his shoulder to make sure nobody was listening. 'Did you come up with a name for it?'

Dylan swallowed the last mouthful of his cereal bar. 'Have you forgotten who you're talking to?' he said with a wink.

Freddie folded his arms. 'Okay then *word wizard*, tell me!'

'Not yet - but I promise you'll love it!' said Dylan, setting off down the road.

When they arrived at the gatehouse, Tiny Tom gave them both a big shiny golden smile. 'Hi lads! Dave's on his way down, he won't be a minute.'

Dylan peered into the gatehouse. 'Hi Tiny Tom! How did you get on with your scarf?'

'It's finished!' he replied, pulling a large knitted multicoloured scarf out of a bag.

'Obviously, the holes are supposed to be there. For ventilation purposes, you know. I'm now trying my hand at embroidery. Check this out, I've made Rock Star's face! What do you reckon?'

The friends looked at the round disk being held out in front of them. Freddie thought it looked more like a pizza than a face. Tiny Tom was definitely better at knitting, and that was saying something.

'It's colourful!' blurted Freddie, aware that Dylan's answer might not be as kind – or make as much sense.

As the gates swung open, Dave rode through on his buggy.

'Hi boys! Hop on and I'll take you up.'

They gave Dave a smile and both climbed on. Freddie rested the rucksack across his knees, while Dylan sat cracking his knuckles one by one all the way to Rock Star's mansion. When they walked inside, Dave showed them once again into 'Star's Bar', where Cheryl was waiting for them.

'Would you like a drink?' asked Dave. 'The boss was finishing his tennis lesson when I left, so he'll be here any time now.'

Dylan walked along the line of old arcade games. 'Two whisky and lemonades please, Cheryl - without the whisky!'

Freddie walked to the window and looked down at the statue of Rock Star playing his guitar. The wheezing man staggering into the room didn't look a bit like the statue.

'Now then, boys!' gasped Rock Star, trying to catch his breath. His cheeks were bright red, and his white shorts showed off a pair of knobbly knees covered in grass stains.

'How was your tennis lesson, Rock Rats?' asked Dylan.

Rock Star scrunched up his face. 'Torture! I hated every minute. I've told my coach to get his hands on some tennis balls that move as slowly as I do before next week. Why anyone *enjoys* chasing a little yellow ball of fluff all over the place is completely beyond me! Freddie, have you brought me some more of your mum's delicious soup?'

'I have,' said Freddie, emptying his rucksack. 'There's the one you tried before, in your big flask – and then there's this...'

Freddie held up his dad's small tartan flask.

Rock Star's eyes lit up. 'Ooh, what do we have here?'

Freddie smiled. 'I told mum about what you wanted. 'Like stinky cheese, no dairy, anything goes' and she's done it!'

Dylan scrunched his face.

'Well then, what are we waiting for?' said Rock Star.

Cheryl disappeared out of sight, returning a moment later with a bowl and spoon on a small silver tray. Rock Star clapped his hands together.

'I haven't been this excited since I performed for the Queen in '98! Right then Freddie, *sock it to me!*'

CHAPTER 23 - KCOS

Wasting no time at all, Freddie poured some of the soup into the bowl. Rock Star lifted it up to his nose, closed his eyes and took a long deep sniff. He popped a large spoonful into his mouth, swished it, swoshed it, and swallowed it. Freddie and Dylan waited nervously.

'Whoah, man, this is the business!' exclaimed Rock Star. 'Are you sure this is dairy free? No cheese whatsoever?'

'No cheese whatsoever,' said Freddie proudly. 'Mum takes these things *very* seriously.'

Throwing the spoon onto the tray, Rock Star grabbed the flask and tipped out a second helping. He lifted the bowl to his mouth and finished the lot in a flash, wiping his mouth with the back of his hand.

'I honestly can't believe it,' gushed Rock Star. 'This stuff is amazing, it's like I'm totally *drinking* stinky cheese. Your mum is a *genius!*'

Freddie looked over at his friend who was looking paler by the minute.

'Dave, wanna try some?' asked Rock Star.

Freddie and Dylan glanced at each other as they waited for Dave's reply.

'No mate! You tuck in,' said Dave, giving the flask a sniff. 'Wow, what's in this stuff?'

Freddie stepped forward. 'She said it's a rare and unusual ingredient, high in minerals. She found it somewhere... down south.'

Rock Star looked intrigued. 'Down south, eh? What's it called?'

Freddie quickly looked to Dylan for help.

'Kcos,' said Dylan.

'Cos *what*?' said Rock Star, confused.

'No, that's the name of the ingredient, *Kcos*!'

'Cos *what's* the name of the ingredient? I'm lost!'

Dylan opened his mouth to reply, but Rock Star raised his hand. 'Well, whatever it is, I don't care. I love it! I can't believe I'm not eating the real thing. There's only one way to know for sure!'

Freddie felt a sudden rush of nerves. 'What's that?'

'If there *is* any cheese in it, in half an hour my bottom's going to explode and you'll be running for cover! Tell you what, let's have a game of something and wait to see if anything... *happens*. Who's for darts?'

The boys nodded in agreement. Rock Star looked in the direction of the bar.

'Come join us, Dave! Hey Cheryl, I don't suppose you fancy a game too?'

Cheryl threw down the cloth and smiled. 'I thought you'd never ask.'

'I'm only going to join you if you play properly!' added Dave.

'What do you mean *properly*?' asked Freddie.

'He means this,' said Rock Star, picking up a dart and throwing it in the general direction of the dartboard.

As the dart flew through the air, the dartboard *moved*. The whole board shifted up and left, and the dart landed in the centre of the bullseye.

'Coooooool!' uttered Freddie.

Dylan edged closer to the dartboard. 'Punch my pickle! Do that again, Rock Star!'

This time, Rock Star turned away from the dartboard and threw the dart over his shoulder. The dartboard dropped down and right, with the same result – a perfect bullseye.

Rock Star smiled. 'What can I say, I like my gadgets!' He flicked a small switch on the side of the board. 'Fine, I'll play the *boring* way – but be gentle. I haven't had a proper game in ages. I normally play against Tiny Tom, and he needs the board's help more than *I* do. His arms are so huge he can't throw a dart straight, it's like playing darts with a chicken. Poor guy has to throw it sideways like a frisbee. Right, nearest the bull starts. Ladies first! Cheryl, let me know if you need any tips…'

Cheryl stepped up to the mark on the floor and threw her first dart. With no help from the dartboard, it landed straight in the bullseye. The twinkle in her eye said it all.

After Cheryl had beaten them all for the third game in a row, Rock Star shook her hand. 'You kept that quiet, Cheryl – I didn't know you could play?'

'You never asked,' replied Cheryl, 'I'm the captain of the local darts team. I play a mean game of pool too; I practice on my lunch break.'

Rock Star rubbed his chin. 'Fancy a change in your job description? I'd love for you to teach me.'

'Sounds great,' said Cheryl, heading back to the bar with a smile.

Rock Star looked down at his watch. 'Well, Freddie - your mum was telling the truth. I'm an explosion free zone! I don't know how she's done it. I need this in my life, and lots of it too! You'll have to let us know how we can pay her for more. So, does this new one have a name?'

'Oh yes,' said Dylan. 'It's called 'Rock Stock'.'

'*Rock Stock*?' chuckled Rock Star. 'I love it! Oh, and Freddie? Tell your mum from me, if she gets the chance to make any more versions, keep them coming. This stuff's amazing!'

CHAPTER 24 – THE MUM-SHAPED BULLET

'Cos?' asked Freddie.

An hour earlier, the best friends had been playing darts with a world-famous rock legend in a huge mansion. Now they were sitting in Freddie's back garden, playing fetch with Flash, and enjoying a well-earned ice cream.

'With a K! It's 'sock' backwards,' Dylan added with a wink.

'Genius!' replied Freddie. 'Oh, and the name, 'Rock Stock'? I love it. What a team!' Freddie licked his ice cream and smiled.

Dylan heard his mum shouting from the back door. He swiftly demolished the last mouthful of ice cream and squeezed through the hole in the fence. Seconds later, Freddie heard a squeal coming from his mum's window, closely followed by the creak of their stairs. His mum raced into the garden, her squelching socks leaving wet footprints across the patio. She looked like she was going to burst with excitement.

'Freddie, you'll never guess what! Someone's donated £300 through my 'buy me a coffee' link. That's one heck of a big coffee! Isn't that fantastic?'

'£300?' Freddie nearly choked on his ice cream. That was faster than he expected. He hoped Rock Star hadn't dropped him in it. 'Any idea who it's from?' asked Freddie, his heart racing.

'Not a clue, it's anonymous. I've been speaking to a few new people through my helpline this week, and some of them are very grateful, but I wasn't expecting that! I wonder who it was?'

Freddie breathed a sigh of relief. 'Who cares! That's totally brilliant, mum. You should be really proud of yourself.'

'Thanks son!' she replied, ruffling his hair. 'Right, time to change my socks again. It's a hot one today! In fact, I think I'll treat myself to an ice cream too.'

Freddie watched his mum disappear back inside. He popped the last bite of ice cream in his mouth, closed his eyes and smiled in the direction of the sun.

The knock on the front door came as his mum was in the kitchen. Seconds later, he'd wished he'd answered it himself.

Hearing the familiar voice, he raced inside to find Dave on the doorstep. He was holding a bag in his hand. 'Hi Freddie! I forgot to give you this strawberry net when you dropped the soup off. I thought it might help.'

'Er, thanks Dave,' winced Freddie, wanting the ground to swallow him up. This wasn't good. Freddie took the net and fiddled with it while his mind raced.

His mum folded her arms. 'And you are?'

Freddie had to think quickly. He'd told his mum he was taking the soup for his teacher – a teacher his mum had never met. If he worded it carefully…

'Mum, this is Dave. Dave's the one that asked us to drop off that soup challenge this morning, remember?'

'Oh, right.' She turned back to Dave. 'The soup. Or, as I like to call it, dishwasher juice!'

Dave looked puzzled. 'Dishwasher juice?'

'Can't stand the stuff,' she replied, scrunching her face. 'Hi, I'm Freddie's mum, Kate. So, was the soup a success?'

Dave opened his mouth to reply, but Freddie butted straight in. 'I'll tell you about it later. Thanks for the net, Dave,' snapped Freddie, desperate to end the conversation.

'See you next week, then, Freddie...' were the only words Dave managed to say before the door closed. The last thing Freddie saw was a very confused expression on Dave's face.

His mum turned away from the door. 'Since when did you start calling teachers by their first name? And why on earth was he dropping a net off for you?'

Freddie walked in the direction of the kitchen so she couldn't see his face. 'He's a very relaxed teacher. I told him about the strawberries on Dad's veg patch,' winced Freddie, hoping his mum believed him.

'Ah, I see. That's kind of him,' she replied, looking back in the direction of the front door. 'I'm sure I'd have paid more interest at school if my teachers had looked like him!'

Freddie cringed before allowing himself to breathe a huge sigh of relief. He'd dodged a huge mum-shaped bullet, but had he upset Dave in the process? He had a whole week of waiting – and cooking – until he could find out.

CHAPTER 25 - THE ICE CREAM JUKEBOX

'Sorry about last week, Dave,' said Freddie, nervously handing over two large sloshing flasks.

His fears were answered with a smile.

'It's fine, Freddie. It was great to meet your mum, too.' Dave jumped on the buggy and beckoned for the boys to follow. 'Hop on, I'll take you to see the main man. He's full of energy this week - he's even been exercising! Come and see for yourselves...'

Freddie and Dylan found their famous friend enjoying the sunshine, swimming in his guitar shaped swimming pool. They couldn't believe their eyes.

'Smash a satsuma, Rock Rats!' blurted Dylan, his mouth wide open.

Rock Star swam over to a large inflatable microphone and

grabbed his sparkly sunglasses. "Hi lads! Like my pool? I used to have it filled with Champagne. I thought it would be amazing, but it was impossible to swim in! The bubbles kept going up my nose, my eyes stung like crazy, and I ended up all sticky. I sank to the bottom once; my medallions were heavier than I thought. Poor Cheryl had to jump in and rescue me. Now it's filled with the usual stuff, and I couldn't be happier. I've been in it three times this week – *three times*! I even went for a couple of jogs with Dave. I don't know what's going on, but I'm feeling so much better!'

Rock Star pointed in the direction of an old jukebox.

'Why don't you treat yourself to an ice cream, and I'll be over in a flash.'

Freddie stepped forward for a closer look. He'd seen the old jukebox in Star's Bar, filled with old vinyl records – but this one was filled with something completely different. Freddie couldn't believe his eyes.

'Squeeze my spots, I'm in love!' exclaimed Dylan.

Rock Star jumped out of the pool and dried himself off. He threw on his sparkly black tracksuit and jogged over to join them.

'Say hello to my ice cream jukebox! It was the first thing I asked my designer to make. I've had it years! You choose a flavour from the list, then pick how you want it – tub, cone, sprinkles... you get the idea. It's got all the *normal* flavours like strawberry, vanilla, and mint choc chip, then there's all my old favourites. It's a shame I can't have them anymore, what with my dairy intolerance and all, but I can't bring myself to get rid of it.'

Freddie scanned the ice cream flavours. There were so many he wasn't expecting - fish and chip flavour ice cream, pizza, cheeseburger and chips, fried chicken – even guitar flavour ice cream, complete with bits of guitar string sticking out the sides.

Rock Star sighed and stroked the glass. 'What I wouldn't give right now for a good old microphone and drum kit ice cream. Ah well, tuck in lads. It's a shame to see it go to waste!'

Freddie chose tikka masala ice cream, and Dylan chose a double scoop – doner kebab and bubble-gum with extra sprinkles. Rock Star pressed a couple of buttons, and the boys watched in awe as two perfect cones appeared out of the front of the jukebox.

'This is so cool!' exclaimed Freddie.

Rock Star smiled. 'I'm going to ask my designer to make me another jukebox, but this one I want to fill with your mum's Rock Stock. Has she managed to come up with any new flavours, Freddie?'

Freddie glanced over at Dylan before replying.

'Not yet, but she's working on it.'

'Brilliant news,' replied Rock Star. 'Tell her to put some welly into it and step-up production. I'd love some new Rock Stock flavours, and I don't care how much it costs.' Rock Star looked at the ice cream jukebox machine one more time before turning in the direction of his mansion.

'Right, boys! Who's for a game of pool?'

CHAPTER 26 – THE BRAINWAVE

Later that afternoon, the best friends sat in Freddie's garden, throwing a very soggy ball to an incredibly happy Flash. After a few minutes, Freddie suddenly sat up straight.

'Hey Dylan, I've had an idea!' said Freddie excitedly.

Dylan cringed. 'Oh no, not again!'

'You know Rock Star wants 'my mum' to come up with some new flavours? Well, I was thinking about what he said, you know, about 'putting some welly into it'. Well, why don't we?'

'What are you on about?' asked Dylan.

'We could use Mum's wellies! Mate, they're the smelliest footwear she has!'

Dylan's eyes widened. 'It's a phrase, Freddie! Something people say, like 'put some effort in'! He didn't mean put a real-life *welly* in it!'

Freddie shuffled forward. 'Why not? Then there's her trainers, slippers – all sorts, and they all have one thing in common. Mum's cheesy feet!'

Dylan cringed. 'Freddie, are you thinking what I *think* you're thinking?'

Freddie raised his eyebrows. '*I'm* thinking I've come up with a plan for more Rock Stock flavours!'

Dylan gulped. 'I don't know whether I should be happy or terrified...'

'Isn't it brilliant?' added Freddie, hardly listening to his friend. 'All we'd have to do is clean the bottoms of the shoes, so they're not covered in something grim like dog poo, then I can chuck them in the pan with the rest of the ingredients. If Rock Star likes mum's sock juice, he'll go *crazy* for her *slipper* juice!'

'Ssssslipper juice?' shuddered Dylan.

'Absolutely!' replied Freddie. 'So - wellies, slippers and trainers are the obvious ones to go on the list, as they're even smelly on *normal* people. What else?'

Dylan turned a funny shade of green.

'I know,' said Freddie, 'mum's got some fancy shoes at the

bottom of her wardrobe, from when she used to go out with Dad. She hasn't worn them in years.'

'*Ytsat*,' Dylan replied, puffing out his cheeks and holding his stomach.

Freddie laughed. 'They'll be nice and mature, like cheese! We could try her flip flops and crocs too. They're not as sweaty, but she wears them a lot!'

Flash made a whimpering noise and ran up the garden.

'All we need to do now is wait for a mum-free day,' said Freddie. 'I can't wash all her shoes without her noticing. We'll need a few hours, and lots of sunshine to dry everything.'

'Bit tricky when she only ever goes out to see your gran,' said Dylan.

'Leave it with me,' said Freddie, 'I'll think of something'.

CHAPTER 27 - THE MEGA-TRIAL

The next few weeks flew by, with deliveries of Rock Stock taking place every weekend. The summer holidays were here, which meant they could spend more time playing pool and darts and hanging out with Rock Star, Tiny Tom, Cheryl and Dave.

Freddie finally had the perfect day to run the 'mega-trial', as Dylan called it. Freddie's mum was going to be out all day at his gran's, the weather was perfect for drying, and they had a long list of footwear ready to go.

Freddie watched from his bedroom window as his mum walked down the road. She was heading off to paint the walls inside gran's summer house. Gran had requested something to do with 'Route 66'. According to his gran, Route 66 was a super-long road in America that she had always dreamed of riding across, on some big old motorbike. For a moment, Freddie stood thinking about how his gran had finally lost the plot – until he realised that *he* was the one spending the day *boiling his mum's footwear to turn into soup for a famous rock star with no stomach.*

As soon as his mum was out of sight, Freddie ran downstairs into the kitchen. Dylan was already making his way up the garden. Thirty minutes later, Freddie had most of the ingredients prepped on the kitchen worktop and Dylan had the most important ingredient - the footwear - neatly lined up outside. Freddie looked at the checklist he'd written late last night.

'Okay, I'm going to make one large pot of Rock Star's normal soup, before splitting it into smaller pans and adding the *special ingredients.* That way we can hopefully get everything cooked and out of the way in two shifts, giving us time to hide the evidence. We'll start with the footwear that will take the longest to dry – trainers, wellies, slippers and socks. We'll then do the flip flops and crocs, and mum's stilettos and wedges from her wardrobe. OK?'

'As long as there's ekac to keep me going, all this work's going to make me extra hungry!' Dylan replied.

'Don't worry,' said Freddie, 'I've made you plenty of cake. Right, let's make a start. You get cleaning the bottom of those wellies, and I'll get cooking.'

Five hours, four pans and eight lots of footwear later, the boys fell into a heap on the grass. A long row of footwear was hanging from the washing line, drip-drip-dripping in the bright sunshine. Flash was laid in the shade, fast asleep.

'My nose is on fire,' said Dylan.

'I can't feel my tongue,' said Freddie.

'I think I've gone colour blind,' added Dylan.

'But we did it!' announced Freddie, 'Seven brand new versions of Rock Stock!'

Dylan held his breath, ran back inside, cut himself a piece of cake and sat back on the ground next to his friend.

'Let's take them tomorrow and see what Rock Rats thinks,' said Dylan, licking his lips and lifting the cake to his mouth.

Freddie sat up and smiled. 'You know, when I used to dream

about cooking for someone famous, I was thinking more like *sticky toffee pudding*, not *sticky slipper soup!*'

Dylan stopped in his tracks, puffed his cheeks out and put the cake back down on the plate.

Freddie burst out laughing. He couldn't wait to see what Rock Star thought of the 'new versions of Rock Stock', aka his mum's footwear collection.

CHAPTER 28 - SNOTGNILLEW

Cheryl walked in carefully carrying a large silver tray covered in bowls and spoons.

'Whoah, I haven't been this excited since I played Live Aid!' exclaimed Rock Star, rubbing his hands together.

'Can Dylan take some notes?' asked Freddie. 'For mum?'

'Sure. What do you need from me?' asked Rock Star, spoon in hand.

'Describe what it tastes like, what it reminds you of, that sort of thing,' said Dylan, feeling nauseous at the thought of what Rock Star was about to try.

'Happy to help,' replied Rock Star, diving the spoon straight into the first tub.

'So, this one's your usual flavour,' said Freddie, 'the original Rock Stock.'

Dylan winced at the smell of Freddie's mum's sock juice.

'Yeah, I love this one, so ripe and cheesy,' replied Rock Star, savouring the flavour. 'It's got such a *familiar* taste, but I can't quite put my finger on it...'

'Or toe!' muttered Dylan under his breath, swiftly elbowed by his friend.

'Right,' said Freddie nervously, 'this is Rock Stock number two, we hope you like it!'

Dylan looked down at the list on his phone. He'd named this one 'Snotgnillew', which was 'wellingtons' backwards. He'd had nightmares about those wellies, especially as he'd had to clean them. Rock Star took a big mouthful and whole face lit up.

'Oh, man, that's delicious! Such a deep, earthy cheesy flavour, with a hint of rubbery seafood. It tastes kind of like cheesy squid. I love it!'

At the end of the session, Dylan handed a very relieved Freddie his list of notes. He scrolled down the rest of the page:

Rock Stock 3 – 'Sreppils' – secret ingredient Slippers

More delicate, a soft cheesy bedtime drink. Gentle on the palate.

Rock Stock 4 – 'Spolf Pilf' – secret ingredient Flip Flops

Fun, light, cheesy cocktail flavour, perfect for the pool.

Rock Stock 5 – aka 'Segdew' – secret ingredient Wedges

Tastes like a stinky cheese sandwich. Cheesy cork flavour, perfect with red wine.

Rock Stock 6 – aka 'Sottelits' – secret ingredient Stilettos

Punchy little number, with a cheesy sharpness. Might cause headaches.

Rock Stock 7 – aka 'Sreniart' – secret ingredient Trainers

Great all-rounder, ideal for a morning. Kick-starts the day.

Rock Stock 8 – aka 'Scorc' – secret ingredient Crocs

Strong, pure cheesy smell. Not one for the faint hearted. Has a real bite.

Rock Star walked over and patted Freddie on the back. 'Well, I'd call that a success, I don't know how she does it!'

'Me neither,' replied Freddie, trying not to think of what his mum would say – and do - if she knew what her son was doing right this minute.

'Please tell your mum I'll be sending her a bonus for these samples to say thank you, and if it's okay with her I'd like to order the lot! I hope she can get her hands on enough ingredients. Are these from the same place? Somewhere down south, wasn't it?'

Dylan had to bite the insides of his mouth to stop himself from laughing.

'Down south, yes,' replied Freddie, trying not to look at his friend. 'Same area, same core ingredients, but different *versions*?'

It came out as more of a question than an answer, but Rock Star didn't notice. He was the happiest they'd ever seen him.

'Well, you tell her from me, she needs to put her *foot* down because I'm going to be wanting plenty of these bad boys! I can't get over how much energy I have, and it's all since you started bringing me your mum's soup. I'm jogging with Dave every morning and playing tennis every afternoon; I feel like a new man! Hey, it's not just me that's changed either, my designer has finally finished renovating the west wing! Want a guided tour while you're here?'

Freddie was more than happy to change the subject. 'Yes please!'

'Lead the way, *Rock Rats*!' said Dylan.

Rock Star set off in a brisk walk. 'If you think my ice cream jukebox is cool, wait til you see this lot!'

CHAPTER 29 – SIC

After walking down a long corridor, Rock Star smiled and swung open the door. Freddie looked first and couldn't believe his eyes. Rock Star now had his own cinema, currently showing an old Disney film.

'Isn't it great?' said Rock Star, 'I used to love going to the cinema when I was growing up, but it's a nightmare when you're famous. So, I thought if I can't go to the *cinema*, the cinema can come to me!'

Dylan stepped inside for a closer look. 'Juggle a jigsaw, this is amazing!'

A voice from the front row made them jump. 'Shhhhhhhhh! This is the best bit!'

They saw a figure stand up and turn around, wiping their eyes. Freddie squinted to try and make out who it was. The giant trembling shoulders and gold teeth gave it away.

'Sorry!' whispered Rock Star. The three of them quietly made their way out of the room and closed the door. 'Oh man, Tiny Tom's such a softie. He looks like he'd break your neck, but put a Disney film on and he's in bits!'

The next room they were taken to came as quite a surprise – it was made up entirely of trampolines. There were trampolines on the floor, on the walls and even on the ceiling.

'This is my trampoline room,' announced Rock Star. 'Exercise should be enjoyable. Dave tried to get me skipping – I told him I'm not six! So, I had my designer work their magic. Twenty minutes of bouncing and you'll feel like you've climbed a mountain, but it's much more fun. Give it a try!'

Freddie and Dylan kicked off their trainers and stepped onto the first trampoline. Within seconds, they were bouncing each other off the walls and howling with laughter. Rock Star flicked a switch on the wall and the floor slowly tipped to one side. Freddie noticed that the whole room was spinning – not in a *feeling dizzy* way, but in a *real* way.

'Don't worry,' shouted Rock Star, 'you'll get used to it. The whole room rotates, so in 30 seconds the floor will be the ceiling and the ceiling will be the floor. Isn't it cool!'

The boys looked like they were going to burst with excitement as they bounced higher and higher.

'I don't know how much you pay your designer,' said Freddie, 'but it's not enough!'

Dylan nodded while he bounced. 'Too right! This is *sic*!'

'What's that?' asked Rock Star, 'You're gonna be sick?'

'No!' chuckled Freddie. 'It's an expression! It means it's cool!'

'Why didn't you say that?' said Rock Star, shaking his head. 'I thought I was going to have to get the cleaners in! Well, if you think *this* room is sick, or vomit, or whatever you kids say these days, you're gonna love the next one!'

CHAPTER 30 - SUPERCAR TURNTABLE

The boys slipped their trainers on, looked at each other and laughed – they were both bright red and their hair was sticking to their heads. Rock Star set off again down a long corridor and they had to run to keep up with him. When he eventually stopped, Rock Star turned round and folded his arms. 'This is my *favourite* new toy. Boys, I'd like to introduce you to my *supercar turntable!*'

'Cuddle a cactus,' said Dylan, grabbing Freddie's arm. 'I've died and gone to heaven!'

In front of them were supercars that most people could only ever dream of. Dylan recognised some of the cars from his dad's wall calendar. He spotted a red Ferrari, a yellow Lamborghini, a black Aston Martin, a silver Porsche, a gold Maserati, and finally Dylan's dream car - a bright blue

McLaren. They were all parked in a circle, facing outwards. Rock Star picked up a small remote control and pressed a button. The circular floor started revolving and the boys stared in disbelief as each supercar passed by.

Rock Star jumped onto the turntable and walked to the centre. 'I had this whole turntable made to look like a giant record, so now the world's *greatest cars* are resting on my *greatest hits*! Sometimes I close my eyes and play 'musical cars' – when I take my finger off the remote, whichever car is in front of me is taken for a spin!'

Freddie shook his head. 'You're the luckiest person alive!'

Rock Star smiled, but seconds later he was shrugging his shoulders.

'You'd think so, wouldn't you? Don't get me wrong, I know I'm lucky in so many ways. I've lived an extraordinary life. I've met some amazing people and I've got lots of cool toys, but I've missed out on *other* things. Things that *normal* people do – like getting married, having kids, you know? The simple stuff.'

Rock Star looked at his watch.

'Oh, man! Is that the time? Sorry boys, I've gotta go! That

Mark Dooley from the newspaper has talked me into doing another interview. Face to face this time, heaven help me. It's the first one since my accident, and it's going out live on their YouTube channel. I'm not looking forward to it. Last time I was on camera, I looked so different. Now when I look in the mirror, all I see is my dad!'

'Couldn't you say no?' asked Freddie.

'If only it was that simple,' sighed Rock Star. 'Now then, are you sure your mum wouldn't like a mention while I'm on? Most people would love a shout-out on TV!'

Freddie's eyes widened and he shook his head. 'Please don't, she *hates* that stuff. What she likes is for people to 'pay it forward'... you know, if you do a good deed for someone, they do something nice for someone else, and it keeps going.'

'Hmmm, 'pay it forward', eh?' said Rock Star, rubbing his chin, 'We'll have to see what we can do about that, won't we?'.

CHAPTER 31 - EXCLUSIVE INTERVIEW

Freddie's heart was racing with nerves. Looking out of the window at Star's Bar he watched as a camera crew set up equipment near Rock Star's fountain. When Tiny Tom moved, Freddie saw an odd-looking man with a microphone. He realised he was finally looking at Mark Dooley, the reporter who had hurt and embarrassed his mum.

The man definitely shared some rodent-like qualities. He had a long pointy nose and rotten teeth. He was nearly bald, except for several wispy long hairs that were dancing around in the breeze like loose puppet strings. He wore a crumpled shirt and tie and had rings of sweat under both armpits. He looked like he was trying to smile, but it was more of a sneer.

When it was time for the interview to start, Cheryl called the boys over to the bar. A huge screen slowly dropped down from the ceiling. They all watched intently as Rock Star appeared on the screen – and live around the world. Freddie crossed his fingers and hoped Rock Star wouldn't drop them in it. Before long they heard a whiny voice.

(MARK DOOLEY) 'Hello. I'm award-winning reporter Mark Dooley. I'm here with another Rock Star world exclusive for The Pockbury Times. This time, we are going out live on our new YouTube channel from Rock Star's mansion. Earlier this summer I exclusively revealed details of the musician's dramatic surgery last New Years Eve. Surgeons removed a record breaking 36 items from his stomach! It's fair to say that his insides have had a similar renovation to that of his mansion – a complete and utter gutting.'

'So, Rock Star, was this a 'New Year's resolution' to lose some weight? It sounds like you ate a guitar and lost one of your own organs!'

(ROCK STAR) 'That's right, Mark. I did indeed lose an organ. My whole stomach, in fact. I wanted to see the year out in style, and I ended up seeing it out in the back of an ambulance. I wouldn't recommend it!'

(MARK DOOLEY) 'Rock Star, you're famous for your long, curly hair, leather trousers and scary make-up. Tell us, what's with the new look? Or should I say 'old' look?'

(ROCK STAR) 'You know what, Mark? There's a lot of my friends that haven't made it to my age, so I actually count myself lucky. I've been given a second chance at life, and I've decided to embrace it. I mean, who was I kidding? I'm 67, nearly bald, and I was dressing like I was still living in the 1980's. I should have done this years ago!'

(MARK DOOLEY) 'So how are you feeling now, in yourself? Or what's left of you, anyway?'

(ROCK STAR) 'Much better than I was, to be honest. I was feeling quite low after my operation, but when your story went out in the paper, the strangest thing happened. Someone brought me a special gift – a simple homemade soup – and it's changed my life!'

(MARK DOOLEY) 'Really? Did you hear that, listeners? My newspaper has helped to change Rock Star's life! Please, tell our viewers more!'

(ROCK STAR) 'It's like a wonder-soup. My hair's starting

to grow back, and I feel years younger. I'm also enjoying exercise for the first time in my life. Crazy really, I get the same buzz from exercise that I used to get performing to thousands of fans. It's all about the fuel you put in your body, and this soup has turned me from a Ford Fiesta into a Ferrari. I've swapped my pie-ceps for biceps, and I'm even starting to get a six-pack!'

(MARK DOOLEY) 'It sounds like you finally have a stomach to be proud of – on the outside at least. So, Rock Star, can you tell the world any more about this mysterious new soup?'

(ROCK STAR) 'Not really, Mark. All I can say is that it's called 'Rock Stock', and it contains a secret ingredient. The person who makes it wants to remain anonymous. But if it's okay, I'd like to say a special thank-you to them for changing my life. I've heard they're a big fan of 'paying it forward', so I'm going to do exactly that. I've decided to throw a large dinner party for celebrities and locals here at my mansion in their honour. I'm hoping that all the guests will be able to try some of this amazing Rock Stock for themselves – as a starter at my dinner party!'

Dylan looked across at his friend. With Freddie's mouth hanging open, the expression on his face said everything.

CHAPTER 32 - DID YOU SAY 500?

Freddie and Dylan waited until Mark Dooley left before stepping back outside. They found Rock Star stood at the pool bar, finishing off the rest of the new Rock Stock.

'What did you think, boys? Did you watch it?'

'We did thanks,' said Freddie, trying to act cool. 'And thanks for not saying anything about my mum, especially to Mark Dooley. She doesn't like that man at all.'

'Neither do I! You can tell a lot about a man by his handshake, and his is *definitely* more *shake* than *hand*. It was like trying to shake hands with seaweed! And boy does that man love talking about himself! It's like he waits for a pause in the conversation so he can listen to the sound of his own voice again! Why doesn't your mum like him, Freddie?'

'They've got...history,' Freddie replied. 'Mum used to work

at The Pockbury Times. She loved it there, until her boss left to travel the world.'

Rock Star looked surprised. 'Hang on, I thought *Mark Dooley* was the boss?'

'No,' added Freddie, 'it's his mum. She left him in charge and that's when mum said everything changed. He's a real bully, always saying horrible things about people. One day, mum had enough and stood up for herself. He sacked her, then wrote a horrible article about something...something she's embarrassed about.'

Rock star stroked his chin. 'Hmm, that sounds familiar. To be honest, I only agreed to do these interviews because he'd been threatening to post some horrible photos of me after my accident. I thought this would shut him up.'

'But that's blackmail!' blurted Freddie.

'Oh yes. He certainly wasn't happy when I wouldn't tell him who makes it either, *or* what the secret ingredient is. He's now demanding a ticket to my dinner party, but what can I do? Your gran's right, he's definitely a *plank*.'

'So what's this about a dinner party, Rock Rats?' asked

Dylan, tucking into an ice cream.

'Oh yes, isn't it great? It just popped into my head! It's the perfect way to follow in your mum's footsteps and 'pay it forward', don't you think? I'm going to invite my old band mates, and all my *real* friends from around the world that have kept in touch with me since my surgery. There'll be locals too. Freddie, can your mum make an extra big batch of Rock Stock for my guests at this dinner party? I'd love them to try that stuff for themselves. We'll need at least 500 portions!'

'500?' exclaimed Freddie, 'did you say 500?'

'Yeah, I reckon,' said Rock Star. 'There'll be lots of guests, and I'd like some more for a little idea I've got. I'll pay your mum extra of course!'

Freddie shook his head. 'I'm sorry, but I don't think mum could make...'

'I was thinking £5,000?' said Rock Star.

Freddie's eyes looked like they were going to pop out of his head. '*Five thousand pounds?*'

'I know it's a lot to ask,' said Rock Star, 'but it would mean so much to me.'

'I don't know,' said Freddie, 'she'd struggle to make that much of *one* flavour. Maybe if it was a bit of a mix?'

'Like a 'Rock Stock mega mix'?' asked Rock Star. 'That sounds delicious!'

Rock Star shook Freddie's hand before he could reply, then jumped into the pool in all his clothes. 'You've got yourself a deal! Tell your mum that she'd better get cooking, the date for the party is three weeks today. Life's too short to wait! Oh, and one more thing,' said Rock Star as he swam away on his back, 'as I'm inviting locals, both your families have to come - I absolutely insist!'

Suddenly Freddie felt sick. Two questions raced through his mind. How was he going to make that much Rock Stock in three weeks? And how on earth could he stop his mum from coming?

CHAPTER 33 - THE WATCHER

Dave was giving the boys their usual ride back down to the gatehouse on the buggy. He was singing along to the radio, but badly. Freddie thought Dave's singing was even worse than his mums, so he decided to start a conversation.

'Thanks again for the strawberry net, Dave. It's really helped.'

'My pleasure,' Dave replied. 'By the way, how's your mum doing? I haven't seen her since I dropped that net in. I still can't get over how different she sounded in real life. When I first spoke to her on the phone, she sounded so posh!'

Freddie thought about the silly voice Dylan had put on, pretending to be Freddie's mum. Dylan started to chuckle until Freddie kicked him in the shin. 'Yeah,' said Freddie, 'that's mum's phone voice, it's *really* embarrassing. Mums, eh!'

'My mum used to do that too,' said Dave, 'whenever she spoke to her posh relatives. One minute she'd be shouting up the stairs about my fish fingers and beans - the next minute the phone would ring, and she'd turn into The Queen! So, Freddie, is your mum a full-time chef?'

'No, she's an artist,' replied Freddie.

'Wow, that's impressive! What about your Dad? What does he do?'

Freddie looked down at his feet and answered in a timid voice. 'My dad died.'

'I'm sorry,' replied Dave. 'So, when you said it was your Dad's veg patch...'

'I look after it for him,' said Freddie, trying to smile.

'He'd be enormously proud of you. My dad died too, when I was a little older than you. You should keep an eye out for butterflies, Freddie.'

Freddie looked confused. 'Butterflies? Why?'

'Because whenever I see one, I like to think that my dad has come to say hello. I know it sounds crazy, but it brings me comfort. The next time you're out working on your veg patch and you see a butterfly, stop and say 'hello'.'

Freddie could feel his eyes stinging with tears. He blinked them away and muttered a thank you. As they pulled up to the gatehouse, Tiny Tom raced over to Dave and whispered something in his ear.

'Change of plan,' said Dave, quickly setting off back in the direction of the house. 'That new YouTube video's gone viral, which means that lots of TV crews are going to be sniffing round here in no time. Tiny Tom thinks it's best for you to use Rock Star's secret tunnel from now on, and I agree.'

'Secret tunnel? 'Pick my pimples, this place gets *retteb*!' whispered Dylan, who was beaming from ear to ear.

Dave drove the boys round the back of the mansion and past the tennis courts before pulling up outside an old shed. He slid the windowsill to the side, revealing a large red button. As soon as he pressed it, the shed started moving to the left. Freddie and Dylan couldn't believe their eyes. A long tunnel appeared below them with lights running as far as they could see.

Dave turned to face the boys. 'Rock Star used this in the past to get away from the crowds, I never thought we'd be using it for you two!'

Dylan pinched Freddie on the arm.

'Oww! What did you do that for?' asked Freddie, rubbing his sleeve.

'I thought I was dreaming!' said Dylan. 'If you said 'oww', I knew I wasn't!'

Dave pointed down the tunnel. 'Follow the path, and it will bring you out about half a mile past the turning on the main road. It's well hidden in the bushes and covered in an old camouflage net. It's going to be much safer to come this way from now on, so nobody will see you bringing your mum's deliveries. When you come back, wave at the camera, and the shed will move to let you back through. Right, I'll nip back and get your bikes, then you need to get yourself home before we're swamped with TV crews again!'

Freddie couldn't help but smile. A secret tunnel, was there nothing that Rock Star didn't have - other than a fully working stomach?

As the boys raced down the secret tunnel, neither of them had any idea they'd already been seen. Far away in the trees overlooking the gatehouse, the watcher packed his binoculars back into their case and sneered. He didn't know why the two local boys had been driven up to Rock Star's gatehouse, or why they'd disappeared again so quickly. But as he knew where one of them lived, Mark Dooley was determined to find out.

CHAPTER 34 - MARK DOOLEY

Mark Dooley parked up close enough to Freddie's house so that he had a good view, but not close enough that he could easily be spotted. His old silver Ford Fiesta was perfect for missions like this. It was the most common model of car, and the most common colour, which meant it didn't stand out anywhere. Quite like its owner.

Waiting for the boys to arrive home, he realised how hungry he was. He'd not had breakfast, or lunch, and his stomach was growling. He rummaged around in the car door in the hope of finding something edible. On the first attempt, he pulled out a crusty tissue, a broken umbrella and an old parking ticket. He wound down the window and tipped them all onto the road. As his hunt for food was almost over, he found a single boiled sweet down the side of his seat that was covered in fluff and hair. He carefully picked off as much 'stuff' as he could before popping the furry sweet in between his small rotten teeth. His taste buds went into overdrive, and he dribbled down the full length of his crumpled shirt and tie.

Mark Dooley always wore a shirt and tie, whether we was working or not. He even wore them to bed, which is why they were always crumpled, and they always had yellow sweat patches under both armpits. He showered in them too so that he could wash them without taking them off, which he thought was very clever indeed.

Right on cue, Freddie and Dylan swung around the corner and skidded to a stop on their driveways. The reporter wound down his window to try and hear what they were talking about, but Flash barking through the gate had other ideas. According to Mark Dooley's lip-reading skills, it looked like Freddie was saying something about monkey's bottoms, long toenails and tomato ketchup. He knew he had to find a way to get close enough to hear what they were saying.

'I smell something funny going on,' he muttered.

He looked in the rear-view mirror and stared at the face

sneering back at him. Settling back in his seat, he licked the full length of his hand and wet down his few strands of hair. He waited a while longer, passing the time by picking the thick yellow crud from between his teeth with his overgrown fingernails. As there was still no sign of Freddie or his friend, he decided to go back to his flat and eat one of his microwave meals before returning.

As he started his car, he thought of Freddie's mum Kate, and all the horrible things he'd said about her. He sneered as he drove away.

'I'll be back,' muttered Mark Dooley.

CHAPTER 35 - THE DONATION

Freddie could smell what was happening before he walked in through the back door. His mum was tipping a large pan of steaming socks into the sink. As soon as she saw him, she ran over and gave him a wet high five. 'You're not going to believe this!' she squealed, 'I've received my biggest donation yet – *one thousand pounds!*'

'Mum, that's amazing!' said Freddie, in nearly as much shock as his mum. Rock Star mentioned he'd be paying his mum a bonus for the new flavour samples, but he wasn't expecting £1,000! How on earth was she going to react when she received £5,000?

'I know!' she replied with a little dance. 'When I started my Soul Mates website last year, I didn't do it for the money, I did it to help others like me. And now look! I've been racking my brains trying to think who it could be – I mean, £1,000? That's a crazy amount!'

'Maybe one of the people you've helped is some fancy Hollywood film producer?' said Freddie, desperately trying to throw her off the scent.

'I think you must be right! Well, whoever it is, at this rate I'll be able to treat myself to a new vacuum!'

'Or maybe we could go on holiday?' suggested Freddie hopefully.

In an instant, her face changed from super-excited to super-puzzled. She held up something green and droopy over the sink.

'Freddie, check this out - there's some herbs mixed in with my socks!'

Freddie felt his cheeks turning red. 'You must have been near the herb garden, mum. Hey, why don't you let *me* wash your socks from now on? I know how busy you are with your painting and the Soul Mates website and stuff.'

'Thanks, son. You know, the way these donations are coming in, I might even treat myself to some new socks!' She headed outside to hang the socks on the washing line.

'Please don't!' muttered Freddie, thinking how important they now were. He decided to quickly change the subject. 'What time's gran coming?'

'I thought we could go to hers if that's okay with you, chef? Gran's busy gardening, so I thought I could help her while you cook one of your delicious experimental dishes?'

'Cool,' said Freddie. He was looking forward to making something other than soup for a change.

As he gazed into the garden thinking about the challenge that lay ahead, a pretty white butterfly swooped down out of nowhere. He watched as the butterfly circled his mum then fluttered over in his direction, before disappearing as fast as it had appeared. He thought about what Dave said and smiled.

'Love you, dad,' whispered Freddie.

CHAPTER 36 - HIDE AND SEEK

Freddie loved gran's cottage. He loved the family history within those walls. His gran had lived there her whole life, she had been born in one of the upstairs bedrooms. The house was filled with photos, and everywhere you looked there was something special. In the kitchen doorway were small marks with names and dates where family members had been measured over the years. He looked up at his dad's height that was taken on his 18th Birthday and wondered if he'd ever reach that same mark.

The garden was the kind you could get lost in. The only way you could get lost in Freddie's garden was to stand behind the shed - and as his shed didn't have a secret tunnel, games of hide and seek never lasted very long. Here you could spend what felt hours trying to find someone. Hiding in gran's garden was now an essential part of a visit. He would walk in, give his gran a hug, do the usual back-to-back measuring task, then he'd have 60 seconds to run and hide in the garden. That's why Freddie was currently hiding up a tree.

'Too easy,' shouted Freddie's gran, 'I could see the branch moving. Just because I'm old doesn't mean my eyesight's gone!'

Freddie laughed. 'Let's see if you're still as good at finding me in winter when it's dark!'

'Cheeky! Looks like I'll have to invest in some night vision goggles!'

As Freddie climbed down the tree, he caught a glimpse of something unusual out of the corner of his eye. Freddie looked closer. Carved into the tree was a small love heart with some initials. The initials were SS + SS.

'Gran, what's this?' asked Freddie, pointing to the carving.

His gran held her hand over her eyes to shield them from the sunshine. 'Is that still readable?' She paused for a minute and smiled. 'Well, that takes me back!'

Freddie pointed at the letters. 'I'm guessing this is you, SS?'

'Yep, Shirley Sanderson as I was then - before marrying your lovely grandad. That must have been there 50 years! Anyway, get yourself into my kitchen, that 'Mystery Meatball Madness' of yours isn't going to cook itself!'

Walking back home later that evening, Freddie couldn't stop thinking about the love heart that he'd found. He slowed down and linked arms with his mum.

'Spit it out, Freddie. You only do that when you want to ask me something!'

'Mum, have you ever seen a carving on the big oak tree at the top left of gran's garden?'

'I don't think so. What is it?'

'It's a love heart with 'SS+SS' in the middle. I know gran's really cool for her age and everything, but do you think she used to be a bit... odd?'

'*Odd?*' laughed his mum. 'Why would you say that?'

'Putting her own initials in there twice. I mean, I know you keep telling me how important it is to *love* yourself and everything...'

'You daft sausage! Your gran didn't carve that. It was her first boyfriend, before your grandad. They had the same initials,' said Freddie's mum, turning to watch her son's expression. 'Shirley Sanderson + Sid Shufflebottom.'

Freddie stopped in his tracks. 'Sid Shufflebottom?' He couldn't believe what he was hearing. 'But that's Rock Star's real name! You're not telling me that my gran used to go out with Rock Star?'

'Oh yes,' she said with a smile, 'the one and only. She probably wouldn't thank me for telling you, but they used to be childhood sweethearts. Your gran was crazy about him, but he went off to London to chase his dream. Your gran was heartbroken.'

'No way!' replied Freddie, struggling to take it in.

'Yes way! She waited a whole year to see if he was going to come back, but Sid hit the big time. He changed his name, became famous and travelled the world. Then she met your grandad, and the rest is history.'

'Mum, that's crazy! I mean, I knew they were at school together and everything, but I had no idea!' Freddie put his hands on his head. 'Now it all makes sense! Could you imagine if he'd stayed? Or if she'd gone off to London with him?'

'I'm pleased she didn't! Your gran wouldn't have met your grandad, and they wouldn't have had your dad - and that means I wouldn't have *you*.' Freddie's mum squeezed his arm and ruffled his hair.

Freddie smiled and tried to act calm, but his mind was racing. Gran and Rock Star were childhood sweethearts? If gran accepted the invitation to Rock Star's dinner party, it had taken *another* complicated turn.

CHAPTER 37 - WALKING THE DOG

Freddie found his best friend in the front room, watching TV with his mum and dad. The curtains were closed, so Freddie couldn't see much – but there was lots of slurping going on. When his eyes adjusted to the light, he could finally see Dylan's parents. They were sat in their usual chairs with their usual trays, tucking into heaped plates of spaghetti.

Freddie did his best to smile at Dylan's mum, knowing it wouldn't be returned. 'Is Dylan free to take Flash for a walk?'

Dylan's mum checked her watch and muttered something in Welsh. Freddie heard her say 'siomedig' which he knew meant 'disappointing', but he smiled anyway. Dylan jumped up and nearly knocked Freddie over in the rush to get out of the house.

They took their usual route, heading into Sid Shufflebottom

park and aiming straight for their usual bench. They were so busy talking they didn't notice the shadowy figure in the hooded jacket that had been following them.

Freddie unclipped the lead. 'There's a good boy. Off you go!' Flash raced off into the park with his tail wagging furiously. The black and white fluffy bundle of energy was in his element.

Dylan opened a huge packet of crisps, offering them to his friend before sitting on the bench. 'Come on then, what's this *really* about?'

'This stays between us, okay?' said Freddie. 'You're not going to believe this, but Rock Star and gran used to be a *thing*!'

Dylan choked on his crisps. 'Punch a penguin! You've got to be kidding me? Your gran and Rock Rats? Bleurgh!' Dylan pretended to be sick all over Freddie's legs.

'I know, I can't believe it! I found their initials carved up a tree,' said Freddie, drawing a love heart in the air with his finger. 'SS + SS, Shirley Sanderson + Sid Shufflebottom! Mum told me on the way home.'

Dylan laughed before starting to sing, 'Shirley and Sid,

sitting in a tree, K-I-S-S-I-N-G!'

'Eww, stop it!' giggled Freddie, unaware that the hooded figure was now within listening distance just a few feet away.

'This dinner party is going from bad to worse,' said Freddie. 'Now I've got to worry about what Rock Star could say to my gran, as well as my mum. What are we going to do?'

'Simple,' said Dylan, 'we bin the invites before anyone sees them.'

Freddie nodded. 'Good thinking! It's not like they're expecting an invite anyway.'

'It's the only option,' added Dylan with a mouthful of crisps. 'I mean, what will Rock Rats say to your mum if he ends up meeting her?' Dylan stood up and put on his best Rock Star voice. '*Hey, Kate! Thanks for making me all that Rock Stock, man!*' Not to mention what my mum and dad would do if they found out they'd gone there and drunk your mum's *sock juice!*'

'Actually, Dylan, the one for the party isn't just sock juice...'

'Oh yeah, I forgot!' laughed Dylan, putting on his best deep Hollywood-movie-voice. '*Coming soon to a mansion near you, Rock Stock Mega Mix! Starring Kate Wilson's award-*

winningly-stinky feet, and her sweaty, cheesy, stinky socks. Featuring Trainer Juice, Slipper Juice, Croc Juice and... Snotgnillew! Be afraid, be very afraid!'

The rustle from the line of bushes behind the bench made them both jump.

CHAPTER 38 - THE ARGUMENT

Freddie looked up just in time to see the shadowy figure running away. His heart pounded so fast he could feel it through his chest. He sprang up from the bench and looked at his friend.

'No, no, no! Do you think they heard us?' asked Freddie, anxiously.

'Dunno,' said Dylan, finishing off the crisps.

Freddie put his hands on his forehead. 'If they did, I'm dead! Why did you have to say all those things?'

'What?' asked Dylan, shrugging his shoulders.

'All that about mum and her socks and stuff?'

'Hang on!' said Dylan, folding his arms. 'This isn't *my* fault!'

'This is all just one big joke to you, isn't it? Well, I hope you're happy now!' snapped Freddie.

'Happy? Not really mate, no! I *was* happy, before you dragged me into all of this. And what am I getting out of it, Freddie, other than ekac?'

'You're getting way more than cake!' said Freddie angrily. 'You wouldn't have seen the inside of Rock Star's mansion if it wasn't for me!'

'Yeah, but I'm watching *you* living *your* dream,' blurted Dylan. 'What about *mine*?'

Freddie shook his head. 'What? I can't believe I'm hearing this!'

'Me, me, me!' snapped Dylan, getting angrier by the second. 'Is it all you think about? You know I want to be a famous YouTuber, and you won't even let me post the videos of you cooking! Sure, I get why I can't post the Rock Rats stuff, but what about the other stuff you make?'

'You know why!' snapped Freddie, 'because I don't want anyone else knowing about my cooking yet. You know that!'

'And in the meantime I've got hardly any subscribers on my channel, because I can't show the exciting stuff – but I get to film *you* having fun. Yeah, like that's *KO*.'

Freddie rolled his eyes. 'Cos you're not having *any* fun at all, are you? You're not enjoying the pool table, or the ice cream juke box, or the trampoline room, or the cinema...'

'I'm not enjoying all these secrets and lies, Freddie. I hate it!'

'But it's not a secret any more is it, thanks to you and your big mouth! Someone else knows now, and it's all your fault! I know you don't care what people think about you, with all your weird sayings and stuff, but some of us do! You've ruined everything! I hate you!' shouted Freddie.

Freddie ran out of the park with Flash following close behind. He checked Dylan wasn't following before bursting into tears.

Across from the park, the shadowy figure climbed into his car. He dropped the hood on his long black jacket, revealing his crumpled shirt and tie. He took out his mobile phone, pressed play and listened again to the conversation he'd recorded. The sneer on Mark Dooley's face grew bigger, revealing his little rotten teeth, and he spat out one simple word.

'Gotcha!'

CHAPTER 39 - THE INVITATION

Freddie hadn't slept a wink. Instead, he'd laid awake running yesterday's events over and over in his head. In all the years he'd been best friends with Dylan, they'd never fallen out this badly, and it couldn't have happened at a worse time. He couldn't believe what he'd said and had no idea how to take it back. The damage had been done.

Freddie was now trying to work out how he was going to make 500 portions of Rock Stock in only three weeks without his best friend for help.

But the main thing that had kept Freddie awake was wondering who the mysterious figure in the park was. He checked his phone for the hundredth time, terrified that the mysterious figure would have told someone, and that his own face would be all over the news. Fortunately for him, it was still Rock Star's face on every story and not his own. Whoever had heard Freddie and Dylan talking obviously hadn't spoken up yet – but he had a horrible feeling it wasn't going to go away.

Freddie had talked his mum into going round to his gran's house so he could make a start on the Rock Stock for the dinner party. He thought he would have hours to himself, giving him plenty of time to make at least two batches. He was wrong.

The knock on the door made Freddie jump. He turned off the noisy extractor fan and headed down the hallway, hoping the smell hadn't followed him.

'Morning!' said Dave, peering over Freddie's shoulder and sniffing the air. 'Ooh, something smells cheesy! Is your mum cooking some more Rock Stock?'

Freddie pulled the door as closed as he possibly could. 'Yeah, she's making a start for the dinner party.'

'Great!' replied Dave. 'I don't suppose she's free for a chat? I've brought your invitations, and it would be nice to give her them in person.'

Freddie tried to look disappointed. 'What a shame. I'm afraid she's nipped out.'

Suddenly, the sound of the smoke alarm filled the house. Freddie ran into the kitchen and opened the back door. He turned just in time to see Dave's hand on the lid of the pan.

'No!' shouted Freddie, rushing over and slamming the lid back down.

'I was only trying to help,' replied Dave. 'I thought something was burning!'

'Sorry Dave, it's more than my life's worth. Mum gets very funny about people looking in her pans!'

Freddie realised how stupid it sounded the moment he said it.

Dave looked puzzled. 'Your mum really is a character, isn't she? Anyway, here are your invitations to the 'hottest gig in town'. That's you, your mum and your gran. Dylan's invitations are in there too.'

'Thanks,' said Freddie, knowing they would be going in the bin as soon as Dave left.

'Rock Star's looking forward to seeing you all there, and

finally meeting your mum. He's put the six of you on a table at the front. You're in for an amazing night! If there's one thing Rock Star is capable of, it's throwing a party to remember!'

Freddie's heart sank as he heard the familiar sound of his mum.

CHAPTER 40 - THE DROP

'Hi sweetheart, only me. Your gran was out...'

Freddie's mum stopped in her tracks. 'Oh, hello again Dave!' she said, looking confused. She nervously glanced over at the pan bubbling away on the hob. 'What can we do for you?'

'Hi Kate, I'm delivering your tickets for Rock Star's dinner party,' said Dave, pointing at the envelope. 'I hope you and Freddie's gran can make it.'

Freddie's face dropped. There was no way he could bin the tickets now.

His mum took the envelope and lifted out the impressive black and gold invitations while tidying her hair with her free hand.

'Wow! Really?' she replied, reading the names on the invitations. 'Look, Freddie! there's even one for you! That's so kind. Freddie's gran will be thrilled that Rock Star remembers her!'

Dave tilted his head. 'Freddie's gran?'

Freddie's eyes widened.

'Thanks for the invites, Dave!' blurted Freddie, hastily trying to guide Dave out of the kitchen before his mum said anything else.

Dave took the hint and slowly backed out of the room. 'Bye, Kate! I'll look forward to seeing you at the dinner party.' He pointed over at the pan. '*That* smells amazing, by the way!'

When they reached the front door, Freddie followed Dave outside. 'Sorry, I can tell mum's struggling. She pretends she's fine, but it's all an act.'

'Wow, she's very convincing! So, where's Dylan? You two are usually joined at the hip!'

Freddie sighed. 'We fell out,' he mumbled.

Dave put his hand on Freddie's shoulder. 'Sorry to hear that, Freddie. I hope you manage to sort it out. Good friends are worth their weight in gold.'

Freddie tried to smile but failed. 'I said some things. Things

I can't take back.'

'I see,' said Dave. 'If I was you, I'd start by saying sorry and go from there. It's a tough word to say, but it makes a big difference. In fact, you've got the perfect excuse to go round - you can drop off their invites for Rock Star's dinner party! Right, gotta go, lots to do. I'll catch you later!'

Freddie waved Dave off before heading back inside. Suddenly remembering the pan in the kitchen didn't only contain his mum's socks, he raced back into the kitchen terrified he was too late. Fortunately for Freddie, his mum was still stood in exactly the same place, scratching her head and looking puzzled. She pointed in the direction of the pan bubbling away. 'My *pan* smells amazing? I've never heard that one before! And why's a teacher dropping off invites for Rock Star's dinner party?

CHAPTER 41 - COOKERY LESSONS

Freddie tried to think of something fast. 'I think Dave's been giving Rock Star cookery lessons?'

'Cookery lessons, eh?' she folded her arms and started laughing. 'Maybe *you* should go and teach Rock Star a thing or two!'

Freddie gave his best fake laugh.

'I still can't believe we've been invited, Freddie. How about that, eh? Good old Sid Shufflebottom *does* remember your gran after all. I know she wouldn't say it, but she'll be really flattered.'

'But you're not going to go to the dinner party, are you mum?' asked Freddie, cringing. 'I mean, there's going to be so many people there, you wouldn't enjoy it. Maybe we could stay in and watch it together on the TV? I could make your favourite curry?'

Freddie's mum ruffled his scruffy brown hair and smiled. 'It's very sweet of you to look after me, but you know what? I think we should go.'

'No!' blurted Freddie without thinking, quickly followed by 'What I mean is - are you sure you're up to it?'

'Actually, I think I am,' she replied. 'It'll be nice for your gran too. Besides, I've been hiding myself away for too long.'

'Oh, great!' said Freddie, trying to smile when all he wanted to do was cry.

'In fact, I've been thinking. With all these orders for my artwork, and donations through my Soul Mates page - maybe we should go on holiday? A *real* one, not just looking at the paintings on the walls! I'm starting to feel much more confident, and I know you're desperate to travel too. There's a big old world out there, Freddie. What do you think?'

Freddie was speechless, so nodded instead. They hadn't been on holiday for years, and he'd started to feel like they'd never go on one again.

'Right, I'm going to ring your gran and tell her the good

news. I might even see if she fancies a spot of clothes shopping before the big day. I need to find some sweat-proof shoes if I'm going to be mixing with all those famous people!'

She picked up the invitations for Dylan's family and looked confused. 'It's odd that next door has been invited too, but at least you'll have your best friend to hang out with. Talking about Dylan, is he okay? I haven't seen him in a while.'

'Cold,' said Freddie. 'He's got a really bad cold'.

'Bless him. I hope he feels better soon. And I'm sure you'll both have a great time exploring Rock Star's mansion at the party! Do me a favour and give these invites to Dylan the next time you see him. Cheers love!'

Freddie stared at the invitations. Not only did his mum now know about the dinner party, but she was planning to go. This changed *everything.*

CHAPTER 42 - STRESSED

Nearly a week had passed since Freddie and Dylan's argument in the park. The good news was that Freddie's face still wasn't on the news, which meant the mysterious person in the park hadn't said anything - yet. The bad news was that Freddie still hadn't seen Dylan, so his three invitations were currently hidden in a Keith Floyd cookery book. He had no idea what to do with them. In fact, the only person that could give him advice was Dylan, so he was well and truly stuck. Right now, he needed his best friend more than ever.

Freddie's mum was going to be in all day painting, which meant he couldn't risk making another batch of Rock Stock. Fortunately, Freddie had come up with a plan to try and make things right – at least with his best friend - and today was the perfect day to put his plan into action. His plan was called

'*Operation Get Dylan Stressed*'.

Dylan always joked that he loved Freddie making him *stressed*, or in other words, desserts. Freddie had decided to make Dylan's favourite, *ekac*, but with a big difference. He soon found what he was looking for, an image of a 'YouTube play button' plaque. These were an award given to YouTube's most popular channels, something that Dylan dreamed of receiving. Freddie studied the image of the gold version, the plaque given to YouTubers with 1 million subscribers. He put on his bright red apron and bow tie, which his ex-best friend had given him last Christmas, and got to work. He weighed, sieved, chopped, stirred, whisked and baked.

Two hours later he was looking at three large trays of treats, all of them Dylan's favourites. Freddie started by using the large rectangular chocolate cookie as the base and covered it in vanilla frosting. Next, Freddie carefully added the layer of doughnuts with popping candy centre. He smothered them with buttercream before adding the large rectangular layer of chocolate cake to the top.

Freddie then got to work on the play button for the top. He

brushed a silicone triangular mould with melted chocolate. Once that was set, he filled it with marshmallows and jellybeans before covering the top with another layer of melted chocolate to seal it closed. Once it was finished, Freddie gently added it to the top of the cake before covering the whole thing with gold icing.

He threw his bow tie and apron on the table and admired the huge golden 'YouTube play button' in front of him. Freddie hoped this would finally show Dylan how much faith he had in his friend achieving his dreams.

After lunch, he pushed the invitations into his back pocket, took a deep breath and picked up Dylan's cake. Knowing it wouldn't fit through the broken fence panel, Freddie slowly carried the cake up Dylan's driveway. His mouth felt dry, and his heart was racing. The front door opened before he got there. Dylan's mum didn't look happy to see him, but then again, she never did.

'Is Dylan in?' asked Freddie as politely as he could manage.

Dylan's mum stood with her arms folded. 'He said he doesn't want to see you, Freddie. What have you done?'

Freddie looked down at the floor. 'I was an idiot. Said some stuff I shouldn't have.'

'And you think cake's going to fix it, do you?' she replied, looking at the cake and licking her lips. 'What flavour is it, anyway?'

'It's all his favourites,' said Freddie. 'Made into a YouTube play button.'

'A what?' asked Dylan's mum, looking confused.

'It's what he's going to get when he hits a million subscribers on his channel.'

Dylan's mum chuckled. 'Whatever you say!'

'There's these, too,' said Freddie, pulling the invitations out of his back pocket and handing them over.

He could hear her shrieking all the way home.

CHAPTER 43 - JAMES BOND

The days flew by, with Freddie cooking every chance he could get. Today was Friday, the day before the dinner party. There were still no pictures of him on the news, which was a relief, but he still couldn't shake the bad feeling he had.

Freddie still hadn't heard anything from Dylan, even after 'Operation Get Dylan Stressed', so all he could do was hope that by dropping off the invitations he hadn't made matters even worse.

The only good news was that Freddie's mum and gran had decided to treat themselves to a whole day of shopping and pampering, so he had the whole day to do one last big cook. After checking his mum's special box last night, Freddie knew there were at least a dozen sock-shaped flavour bombs ready for action, as well as a whole collection of smelly summer footwear.

His mum and gran were leaving the house at 9am. By 9.10, Freddie was kneeling next to his dad's veg patch, calculating how much he would need for a whole day's cooking. As he dug up some spring onions, he felt another sudden wave of nerves. The white butterfly that fluttered past him made him stop and smile.

'Dad, is that you?' Freddie looked around to make sure that nobody was listening to him having a conversation with a butterfly. 'Look, if it *is* you, and I've not completely lost the plot, I need your help. If you think I should carry on making the soup for Rock Star's dinner party, I need you to land on the peas. If you think I should stop it all right now, land on the beans. Peas or beans, dad. What should I do?'

Freddie held his breath as the butterfly fluttered around his head twice and then disappeared over the house. Freddie sighed. Thinking it must have been someone else's butterfly he carried on collecting the ingredients, trying to focus on how happy his mum would be to receive her £5,000 'donation'.

He spent the next few hours scrubbing, chopping, peeling,

boiling, squeezing and filling. By early afternoon, every container was ready for Dave to collect, and every piece of his mum's footwear was hanging on the washing line. The only thing missing was Dylan. Freddie knew how much fun it would have been with him there, making jokes, sharing chocolate bars and coming out with silly expressions while he filmed. Instead, it felt like one long chore.

When his mum finally arrived back home, Freddie couldn't believe his eyes. Her long scruffy brown hair was now sitting on her shoulders, she was wearing make-up and she smelt like a perfume shop. Dropping her bags on the kitchen table, she gave Freddie a big smile and ruffled his hair. 'How's my favourite person in the whole wide world?'

'Wow!' said Freddie. 'You look amazing, mum. I love your hair!'

She walked over to the mirror and checked out her reflection. 'Do you? Thanks, son. I thought it was about time I treated myself. I even had a makeover!' She turned back to Freddie and smiled. 'You know what? I'm finally starting to feel like *me* again. I know I'm not perfect, but who is? Right now, I feel happy, and confident, and maybe even a little bit incredible. Talking about incredible, check this out!'

Lifting a pretty red dress out of a box, Freddie noticed she had a sparkle in her eyes that he hadn't seen for a long time.

'And this one's for you,' she said with a smile, holding a large bag in his direction. 'Seeing as though you're going to be escorting your glamorous gran and I to Rock Star's dinner, I thought you should look the part. There's something special in there too.'

Freddie peered into the bag. He'd never had a suit before. He ran upstairs and changed as quickly as he could. He looked down, noticing something sparkling on the carpet. In Freddie's hurry to get the suit out, the sparkly black bow tie had fallen out of the bag. He picked it up and smiled - his mum knew him well. He clipped it into place and turned to look in the mirror. The figure staring back at him wasn't Freddie. It was James Bond, license to cook.

His mum was standing in the doorway, wiping away a tear with the back of her hand. It was a sweet moment, right up until she pulled a tissue out of her sleeve and blew her nose.

She had a very loud nose blow that sounded like it came from an elephant.

'Oh sweetheart, look at you. If your dad could see you now! He'd be so proud.'

Looking at his reflection, proud was the last thing that Freddie felt – and he had a feeling it was only going to get much, much worse.

CHAPTER 44 – THE DINNER PARTY

It was finally here, the night of the dinner party. Freddie had never felt so nervous. He'd not slept in days, worrying about all the things that could go wrong.

Dylan hated him, his mum and gran thought they'd been invited to Rock Star's dinner party for the wrong reason, and he was about to watch a whole roomful of people drink soup made from his mum's smelly footwear. He wasn't sure if he was going to hell, or whether he was actually living it. The worst part was that someone out there had heard everything, and there was absolutely nothing he could do about it.

The journey to Rock Star's mansion was very different from the usual. No bikes, and no secret tunnel. This time, Freddie was in a minibus with his mum and gran, Dylan, and Dylan's parents. Dropping off his dad's old flask filled with simple homemade soup seemed like a lifetime ago. Sitting so close to Dylan, who was looking in every direction but his, made the journey even harder.

The minibus pulled up to the gatehouse at 7pm sharp. A security guard they didn't recognise checked their names against a list and waved them through, heading slowly up the road that was so secretly familiar. As they neared the mansion, illuminated by huge spotlights, they pulled up behind a long black limousine with tinted windows. All six of them looked to see who was climbing out of the back and onto the red carpet that ran all the way to the mansion steps. The flashes from the line of cameras lit up their minibus like lightning.

Dylan's mum nearly fell off her seat. 'It's that Welsh singer! You know, the one with the curly hair and lush voice? If he was a chocolate bar, I'd bite his head off!'

Freddie looked round at Dylan in the hope of seeing him smile, but he was gazing out of the opposite window. Finally, the minibus rolled forward, and the door opened. They climbed out and were met by a familiar face. It was Cheryl.

'Welcome to Rock Star's dinner party. May I offer you a

drink?'

Taking an orange juice, Freddie linked arms with his mum and gran and followed the other guests along the red carpet.

They made their way past fire breathers, jugglers, stilt walkers and ice sculptures as lights flashed all around them. They slowly climbed the steps and ventured into the huge hall. It looked so different. There were beams of light bouncing off the walls, while huge bubble machines sent a scurry of perfect bubbles into the air.

The hall was filled with guests laughing and chatting. On the galleried landing, high above the guests, a famous guitarist was playing his latest number one song. Freddie recognised some of the local faces – their butcher, the chemist, the postman – and then there were the celebrities. They were easier to spot. Most of them had super white teeth, orange skin and faces that didn't move when they talked. Some looked like they'd had big black eyebrows tattooed onto their faces. Others looked like their lips had been stung by bees. Freddie was pleased he wasn't a celebrity, it looked painful.

He glanced around at his mum and gran, who were taking in

every detail. He wasn't used to seeing his mum all dressed up, she was normally in jeans with her hair tied back and no make-up on. Even like that she was beautiful. Looking at her now, Freddie thought that she looked like a movie star from the black and white films that his gran loved to watch. Compared to all the other women that were hanging around the entrance, his mum was prettier than them all.

His gran was never one for wearing what she was *expected* to wear. Instead, she was wearing a suit quite similar to Freddie's, but with a few colourful differences. The bright pink waistcoat matched her bright pink hair and her bright pink shoes. She looked amazing, but Freddie had never known her to be so quiet.

Freddie turned to his mum. 'Is gran okay?' he whispered.

His mum smiled and whispered back 'She still can't believe she's been invited. Your gran thought Rock Star had forgotten all about her. She won't say it, but I think she's a bit nervous about seeing him again.'

Freddie nodded and smiled politely, feeling terrible that she'd been tricked into coming. He noticed that his mum's hands were shaking, and suddenly had an idea.

'You sure you're up to this, mum?' he asked, hopefully. 'It's not too late to leave!'

'That's very sweet, Freddie, but I'll be fine. You go and explore with Dylan.'

Freddie's heart sank. Taking a deep breath, he slowly set off in Dylan's direction.

CHAPTER 45 – BAD FEELING

'I'm sorry,' muttered Freddie, the sound drowned out by all the chatter around them.

He cleared his throat and tried again. 'Dylan, mate, I'm sorry. I feel terrible for what I said, I was bang out of order.'

'Yes, you were,' Dylan replied, turning to face him. 'I know you think I don't care what people say, but I do. Especially you.'

Freddie stared at the floor. 'I know you do. I wish there was some way I could make it up to you.'

Dylan kicked the floor. 'Well, there might be *eno* thing!'

'Name it,' said Freddie, 'I'll do anything!'

'KO!' said Dylan, thinking. 'I know. Dance like a chicken. Right here, right now.'

'Are you serious?' asked Freddie, looking around the

crowded room.

Dylan nodded, trying not to laugh.

'Fine,' said Freddie, passing Dylan his drink. 'If that's what it takes...'

Freddie took a deep breath and started to lift his arms.

'*Pots*! I was only messing with you!' laughed Dylan. 'But it's good to know you were willing to do it. Tell you what, how about you make me another ekac instead?'

'Cake?' asked Freddie, looking confused.

'Yeah. Another YouTube one,' said Dylan with a smile, 'but this time make the *diamond play button* – I want to see what my plaque for 10 million subscribers is going to look like!'

Freddie smiled and let out a sigh of relief. 'Deal!'

'By the way, mate, you look really cool in that suit. You look like *Dnob Semaj*!'

'Cheers, Dylan. You too. Now let's go find Dave.'

Dylan followed Freddie through the sea of arms, glasses and handbags. The tall open double doors revealed a room that was bigger than their school hall. It was filled with large round tables. They were covered in white tablecloths with tall flower decorations, guitar ice sculptures and fancy silver buckets with bottles in.

Freddie came to a halt as he noticed something special to the left of the door. In front of them stood a fountain, a small version of the one that stood outside the mansion, with a slowly revolving statue of Rock Star holding his guitar. As he looked closer, Freddie noticed it wasn't water pouring out of the guitar, it was soup. A 'Rock Stock' soup fountain, standing right before their eyes. Dave was right, Rock Star certainly knew how to throw a party.

At the far left of the room was a stage with steps running up either side. Dave was stood in the centre of the stage, tapping on a microphone. The boys raced down the side of the hall and looked up at him in surprise. They'd never seen Dave wearing something so tidy - or clean. Freddie wondered whether Dave's pockets were still full of the *things* that he normally had on him, like a roll of string and a tape measure.

Checking there was nobody around before beckoning Dave to the front of the stage, Freddie spoke quietly.

'Hi Dave, thanks for picking up the rest of the Rock Stock.'

'My pleasure,' said Dave. 'I told the chef to put the lot in one big pan like you suggested. There's enough to feed an army!'

Freddie dropped his voice to a whisper. 'You're sure Rock Star isn't going to say anything about my mum making the soup?'

'Don't worry,' said Dave, 'her secret is safe with us. I'm just pleased you're all here! Right lads, I'll catch you later.'

The friends turned away from the stage and Freddie took a deep breath. At least Rock Star wasn't going to say anything, but something still wasn't right.

'What's up, mate?' asked Dylan, as if he could read his friend's mind.

Freddie's eyes searched the room. 'I've got a bad feeling about tonight.'

'Because of the Rock Stock?' asked Dylan.

'Well, yes, but...'

Dylan looked confused. 'But what?'

'Someone out there heard us in the park, Dylan - I'm sure of it. And they know *everything*. What if they've been waiting for tonight to say something? What if they're here?'

The loud bell ringing in the hallway made them both jump.

'Ladies and gentlemen, please be seated for Rock Star's dinner party.'

CHAPTER 46 - THE TABLE

Freddie found their table where Dave had said it would be. At the front, to the far right of the stage. Rock Star had kept his word. They could see the whole room from where they were going to be sitting.

A stream of guests poured into the room to find their seats. Freddie's mum and gran joined them first, followed by Dylan's parents. In front of each plate was a tiny silver guitar with their names printed on. As they all found their names and sat down, Freddie noticed that their table was made out for 10 people, but there were only 6 of *them*. He jumped as a hand appeared firmly on his shoulder.

'Looks like you've got to put up with me!' came the voice to his right.

Freddie turned and his mouth dropped open. A famous TV

chef was standing right next to him, taking off his jacket and hanging it on the back of the chair.

'Hi, I'm Kevin and this is my partner Sam. And you are?'

Freddie could hardly manage to speak. 'Hi, I'm Freddie. Or at least I think I am....'

Kevin laughed and sat down next to him. 'Nice to meet you,' said Kevin, shaking Freddie's hand. 'So, how do you guys know Rock Star?'

As Freddie tried to think of a reply, his mum leaned over and shook Kevin's hand.

'Hi, I'm Kate, Freddie's mum, and this is his gran, Shirley. Shirley used to know Sid, I mean, Rock Star, years ago.'

'Oh cool!' replied Kevin. 'I used to chef for Rock Star occasionally, back when he could still eat! Apparently, I've been replaced by some local talent who makes this *amazing* 'Rock Stock' soup. Everyone's talking about it, so I thought I'd come and check out the competition. I hope they're here tonight. I've heard they're shy, but I'd love to get some tips!'

Freddie looked across the table at Dylan, who was now sitting next to a YouTube sensation. He must have found it bright inside as he still had his sunglasses on. Instead of a suit, he was wearing a T-shirt from his own merch range, and his girlfriend didn't look very impressed. It was unfortunate for the YouTuber that he hadn't covered his tattoos, as Dylan was having great fun spotting the spelling mistakes.

The guests in the middle of the room starting cheering and applauding, and the noise soon spread through the tables. Rock Star was here. He was dressed in a sparkly black suit with bright pink guitars embroidered down both sides of the jacket. When he turned around, the words 'ROCK STAR' were emblazoned on the back in silver sequins.

'Still a show-off!' tutted Freddie's gran, completely unaware that her own bright pink hair and waistcoat were as much of a fashion statement.

The guitarist headed up onto the stage, while Rock Star walked around the tables shaking hands and greeting his guests. Freddie noticed his gran taking a small mirror out of her handbag and checking herself out, which he'd never seen her do before. As the music played and Rock Star got nearer to the table, Freddie could feel his heart pounding through his shirt.

'Please don't say anything,' muttered Freddie under his breath.

'How are we all doing?' asked Rock Star with a smile, making eye contact with everyone on the table. When his eyes made their way round to Freddie's gran, his face dropped.

'Shirley? Shirley Sanderson? What on earth are you doing here?'

Her face lit up. 'Nice to see you too, Sid, after all these years. Still a joker, I see?'

Rock Star walked round the table, took her hand and gave it a gentle kiss. 'Wow. Look at you! You don't look a day older, Shirl!'

Freddie's gran ruffled Rock Star's short grey hair. 'I can't say the same for you, your name's not the only thing that's changed!' she replied, giggling like a teenager.

Freddie couldn't believe it. His gran was blushing! Her cheeks looked like she'd been running one of her karate classes, they were as pink as her waistcoat. It almost looked like his gran and Rock Star were wearing matching suits.

'I can't believe you're here!' said Rock Star, with his hand on his heart. 'It's so good to see you, Shirl. It really is. Let's catch up later, yeah?'

Freddie watched Rock Star shaking more hands before striding over to his table. There were a few faces Freddie recognised - Cheryl, Tiny Tom and Dave – and a few he didn't. He guessed that the men with big black curly hair must be from Rock Star's old band.

Freddie picked up his menu. There it was in black and white; 'Rock Stock'. Looking around at all the famous movie stars, singers and celebrities, he knew this should have been the best day of his life. He'd always dreamed of cooking for the rich and famous, but not like this.

As he glanced over to the back of the room, Freddie suddenly noticed a pair of eyes staring directly at him. He tried to see who it was, but the room quickly filled with waiters, blocking his view. Freddie's mind raced. He was sure he'd seen those eyes before, but where?

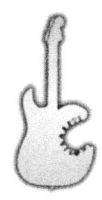

CHAPTER 47 - CHEESY KICK

As Freddie racked his brain trying to think who it could be, a piping hot bowl of Rock Stock soup was placed in front of him. He looked across at his mum and cringed.

Dylan's mum went straight for a basket filled with different shaped bread rolls and *accidentally* dropped a couple into her huge handbag before winking at her husband. Dylan shook his head. Their house was filled with things that had *accidentally* dropped into his mum's handbag – their salt and pepper cellar, their fancy hand cream in the bathroom and half the glasses in their kitchen cupboard.

'Bread roll?' asked Kevin, passing the basket on.

'Thanks,' said Freddie, trying to smile.

In a desperate attempt to take his mind off what they were about to eat, he turned to the TV chef and forced himself to speak. 'I'm a big fan of your show!'

'Cheers mate!' said Kevin, patting Freddie on the shoulder. 'You know, I got into cooking about your age. If you want *my* advice, start with the basics – scrambled egg, jacket potato, that sort of thing - and work your way up. Who knows, maybe one day you'll be lucky enough to cook for people like this!'

Kevin took his first spoonful of soup and sat back in his chair. 'Wow, this Rock Stock is *sensational!* What a mix of flavours!'

'It's totally rad!' said the YouTuber, taking photos of the soup from lots of different angles before turning round and taking some selfies.

'Ooh, this is proper lush,' said Dylan's mum. 'What do you think, Kate?'

Freddie's mum sniffed the soup before delicately tasting a tiny spoonful. 'Freddie knows I normally hate soup - I've always called it dishwasher juice - but something about this is *different*. It tastes almost familiar in some way. It's *really* tasty. I love that cheesy kick!'

Freddie choked when his mum said 'kick' and she patted

him firmly on the back. He looked up just in time to see the eyes staring at him again, only this time he could see their whole face quite clearly. The man in the crumpled shirt pointed slowly at the soup with his spoon, and then pointed at Freddie. He sneered, showing a line of small rotten teeth. In that moment, Freddie knew who had been listening in to their conversation in the park, and it couldn't have been any worse. It was Mark Dooley, and he knew *everything*.

The rest of the meal was a blur. Freddie listened and nodded as everyone said how much they'd enjoyed the 'wonder-soup' that had changed Rock Star's life. He nibbled at his main course of salmon and roasted vegetables. He pushed the berry cheesecake dessert around the plate. He smiled politely and gave one-word answers when anyone asked a question, all the time feeling like the room was spinning. He couldn't help but wonder - what was Mark Dooley's plan?

Coffee was poured into little cups while chocolate truffles were passed around the table. The guests were getting a little louder, which may have been down to the guitarist but was probably due to the wine. Not wanting to make eye contact with Mark Dooley again, Freddie sat wiping the condensation from the side of his glass of lemonade. He took some deep breaths and tried to stop his hands from shaking. Dylan looked over at him and tried his best to give a comforting smile.

Ting, ting, ting!

Everyone looked up as Dave rose to his feet, tapping the side of his glass with a spoon. 'Ladies and gentlemen, your host would like to say a few words.'

Rock Star jumped up from the table in the middle of the front row. As he ran up onto the stage, the guitarist passed Rock Star an electric guitar before waving goodbye and disappearing down the steps. Rock Star pretended to take a bite out of it before playing one of his most favourite guitar solos for the crowd. Everybody cheered. He sipped at a glass of water before addressing his captive audience.

'Friends, celebrities, locals. I'd like to thank you all for coming here this evening. The last time I stood up here with a microphone in my hand, I ate it – and it repeated on me all evening... repeated on me all evening...'

Rock Star chuckled and took a quick drink.

'I think it's fair to say my diet has changed a bit in the last year! Talking about that, I hope you all enjoyed the soup?'

The guests clapped and cheered. Rock Star waited for the noise to die down before continuing.

'What can I say? This Rock Stock has changed my life! I've been asked by so many people this evening what the secret ingredient is, but I honestly don't have the faintest idea...'

'I do!' said a familiar whiny voice from the back of the room.

Freddie didn't need to look to see who had said it. He already knew.

CHAPTER 48 - THE SECRET IS OUT

Mark Dooley swiftly made his way over to the stage, sneering as he walked. The guests muttered between themselves, some of them reaching for their phones. Freddie could feel himself slowly sliding down the back of his chair. He wanted the world to swallow him up.

'What's going on?' asked Rock Star, looking confused.

Tiny Tom and Dave both stood up to see if Rock Star wanted any help, but he waved for them to wait. As Mark Dooley climbed the steps and reached Rock Star, he grabbed the microphone and turned to face the crowd. Everyone was looking at him, which was how he always liked it.

'For those of you who don't know me, I'm Mark Dooley, award-winning reporter for The Pockbury Times. I'm here tonight to share *another* exclusive with you all, and this one's

HUGE! Breaking news, people! I know what the secret ingredient is, *and* I know who makes it too!'

The noise from the crowd grew louder. The YouTuber next to Dylan grabbed his phone, pointed it in the stage's direction and started recording. 'This should be good!'

Freddie could see others were doing the same and froze.

'I don't think we need to do this right now,' said Rock Star, trying to retrieve the microphone. Tiny Tom and Dave started making their way to the side of the stage.

'Oh yes we do,' replied Mark Dooley. 'People deserve to know the truth about what they've eaten here this evening. Ladies and gentlemen, Rock Stock's secret ingredient is… SOCKS!'

The sound of the roomful of guests hearing this news was a mixture of shrieks and sharp intakes of breath. Rock Star stood there in disbelief.

Mark Dooley sneered before continuing. 'That's right, you've all been poisoned here tonight with sweaty, stinky, cheesy sock juice! And do you want to know who by?'

Freddie held his breath, knowing everyone was about to

hear his name.

Mark Dooley paused a second before pointing in their direction. 'Kate Wilson, that's who! The owner of the 'Stinkiest Feet in Town' Award!'

'What?' muttered Freddie, unable to take it in.

Freddie looked over at his mum. The expression on her face said it all.

Mark Dooley performed to the crowd, enjoying every single moment. 'She's been using her award-winningly sweaty feet to give her soup that strong cheesy flavour you've all tasted tonight. Isn't that right, Kate?'

'I don't know what you're talking about,' she pleaded, tears forming in her eyes.

Freddie knew something had to be done, and quickly. He glanced over at Dylan who seemed just as confused. Freddie couldn't stand by and watch Mark Dooley ruin his mum's life a second time. This was all *his* fault, and it was time to stop hiding in the background. Taking a deep breath, Freddie stood up. His legs were trembling underneath him.

'You're wrong!' said Freddie at the top of his voice. 'My

mum's not been making Rock Stock!'

'Liar!' sneered Mark Dooley. 'I heard you and your friend in the park! You said it was made with your mum's sweaty socks! I recorded every word, and I'm publishing it online right now!' He took his phone out, pressed a button and sneered. 'Done! Now the whole world will know what your mum's been up to!'

CHAPTER 49 - THE CHOP

Freddie ran to the bottom of the stage and looked up at Rock Star. He was scratching his head and looking very confused.

'Rock Star, I'm so sorry!' pleaded Freddie. 'It's not mum that's been making it, it's *me*! I only said mum made it because I didn't think you'd try it if you knew the truth. Mum didn't know a thing, I promise. This is all *my* fault!'

The shrieks in the room grew even louder. Freddie turned to face his mum and saw tears running down her cheeks. She looked broken.

'I'm really sorry, mum. I didn't mean for this to get so out of hand, I promise...'

Mark Dooley pointed at Freddie and laughed. 'This gets even better! I mean, what is it with your family? You're as much of a *freak* as your mum!'

Tiny Tom and Dave wrestled the microphone from Mark Dooley, grabbed his arms and carried him down the stairs. As they reached the door, the reporter managed to wrestle himself free. The small tap on his shoulder made him turn around.

'Nobody calls my daughter-in-law a freak!' exclaimed Freddie's gran, karate chopping him across the chest. 'And this one's for my grandson!'. With one swift karate kick, Mark Dooley fell backwards and landed in the Rock Stock soup fountain with a loud 'splosh'. He was covered from head to toe, with soup pouring over him from the statue above.

Some guests were pointing at Mark Dooley and laughing. Others were looking over at Freddie's table and shaking their heads. Before long, guests were grabbing their possessions and scurrying out the room, tapping furiously on their phones.

'One more piece of advice,' said the TV chef, putting his jacket on to leave Freddie's table. 'You might want to stick to the *normal* food groups from now on!'

While Dylan's mum went round the tables *accidentally* finding things to drop into her rapidly expanding handbag, Freddie's mum was sobbing into her hands.

'I'm so sorry mum,' muttered Freddie, not knowing where to look.

'Why Freddie, why?' she cried. 'I can expect hurtful things from Mark Dooley, but you? My own son!' She pulled a tissue out from her handbag, gave her nose a loud blow, and ran out of the room.

His gran ran back over to the table with a scowl on her face. 'Freddie, can you get a lift back with Dylan's family? I need to find your mum and make sure she's okay.'

His gran had never looked at him like that before. Blinking back the tears that were welling up in his eyes, he managed a small nod.

The YouTuber seemed to be the only one enjoying himself as he tapped away on his phone. 'This is awesome! Hashtag 'sock juice', hashtag 'gross', hashtag 'cheesy feet'...'

Dylan *accidentally* knocked the wine all over the YouTuber's legs. '*Spoo*, I'm so sorry, hashtag 'wet your pants', hashtag 'can't spell your own tattoos', hashtag 'your girlfriend's kissing the guitarist'...'

Dylan's mum shuffled back to their table, dragging her

handbag behind her. She tipped the rest of the chocolate truffles into her bag before turning to her husband and speaking in Welsh.

'I do know what that means,' said Freddie, 'and yes, I'm '*disappointed*' in myself too.' Banging his head repeatedly on the table, Freddie listened as the evening crashed down around his ears.

'Come on guys, I'll give you a lift home.'

Freddie looked up in the direction of the familiar friendly voice. Resting on the back of the chair his mum had been sitting on minutes before, Dave was the only one that didn't seem to be trying to make him feel any worse than he already did.

Home. Freddie was not looking forward to going home. Not one bit.

CHAPTER 50 - THE DOORSTEP

Freddie tried his best to talk to his friend on the journey home, but Dylan's mum and dad kept *shushing* him every time he opened his mouth. They climbed out of the back of Dave's car without saying a word, with Dylan managing no more than a squeeze of his friend's shoulder for luck. Freddie sat there in silence, looking at the lights in the hallway and front room and knowing that his mum was inside. He couldn't bring himself to move.

Dave peered through his window in the direction of the lights. 'Do you want me to come to the door with you?'

'Please,' muttered Freddie, trying to hold back tears.

They walked slowly down the driveway, and Dave knocked gently on the door. It was strange for Freddie to be standing at this side of their front door waiting for it to be answered, but he didn't feel brave enough to simply walk in. He heard the familiar sound of his mum blowing her nose before the front door opened slightly. Her eyes were bright red, and she held a tissue in her hand. Ashamed, Freddie looked at the floor and tried to think of something he could say that would make it better. He knew that sorry wasn't going to be a big enough word to make up for the damage he'd caused, but at this moment it was all he had.

'I really am sorry,' pleaded Freddie.

'How could you do that to me?' she asked, wiping her eyes. 'You've taken the one thing you know I'm embarrassed about and turned it into a joke. You've really hurt me.' She sighed and swung the door open. Freddie nervously stepped inside.

She turned towards Dave. 'Can I ask you something? Are you really Freddie's teacher? Food tech, wasn't it Freddie? Apparently, you've been giving Rock Star cookery lessons.'

Dave's face said it all. 'Teacher? Me? No, I work for Rock Star! Have done for years. Why did you think I was a teacher?'

'*More* lies,' she said, shaking her head. 'Sorry, Dave - can we do this another time? Thanks for bringing him home, but I need to talk to my son.' She tried to smile but didn't succeed.

'No problem,' said Dave. 'Look, Kate, I had no idea it was Freddie that was making the soup, or what was going in it. None of us did. Freddie told us that *you* were making it. I don't know why he's done any of this, but I'm sure there's a good reason. He's a good kid with a kind heart.'

As Dave turned and walked back down the drive, Freddie's mum slowly closed the door. Without so much as a glance, she set off down the hallway.

'I still can't believe you'd do such a thing, Freddie. Come into the kitchen, you've got some explaining to do.'

CHAPTER 51 - THE APOLOGY

Freddie took a deep breath, walked into the kitchen and sat across from his mum.

'So why did you do it, Freddie?'

'When I saw that article in the newspaper about Rock Star, I knew I could help him.'

'Mark Dooley strikes again! You're supposed to bin that paper, not read it. You know what that man's done to me.'

'It was all over the internet too, mum. *You* saw it on the telly...'

'And I'm sure you wanting to help Rock Star is nothing to do with the fact that he's famous?' snapped his mum.

'Okay, you got me,' mumbled Freddie, 'but you know I want to be a chef when I'm older, right? Travelling the world, cooking for the rich and famous. It seemed like a great idea at the time. We took him some of my veg patch soup and he loved it.'

'I take it that 'we' means you and Dylan?'

Freddie sighed. 'Yeah, but this is *my* doing, not his. And Rock Star really loved it, mum. He wouldn't have tried it if he thought it was a kid making it, so I said it was a gift from you. He liked it so much he challenged me, I mean you, to make another version.'

Freddie's mum sat back in her chair. 'Is this the soup you told me you were making for your teacher?'

Freddie nodded. 'Rock Star wanted something that tasted *cheesy*,' he cringed, 'but it had to be dairy free. So, I used one of your socks and he loved it. He's been paying you for the soup, and you've been so happy...'

She looked confused. 'Hang on a minute, he's been paying me? How? Oh, I get it. The 'buy me a coffee' donations! All those payments, they were for the soup?' Her eyes filled up again. 'I thought I was making a difference!'

'You were. You are! Look, I know it's a bit weird, but you *have* made a difference. Not only to your Soul Mate guys, but to Rock Star too. He feels so much better and for some reason it's all down to your...' Freddie didn't want to say the words.

'My smelly feet!' said Freddie's mum, pacing around the room. 'Now it all makes sense. The visits from Dave, his weird comment about my pan smelling 'delicious', all that extra money! I thought we'd been invited because of your gran, but it was because of you, wasn't it?'

Freddie tried to reply, but she raised her hand. She gave her nose a loud blow before continuing.

'I thought Rock Star looked more surprised to see her than he should have done. He didn't have a clue that she was coming, did he? Your gran's going to need an apology too, you know. You can't mess with people's feelings like that.'

Freddie felt a tear roll down his cheek. 'I know. I've made the biggest mistake. I really didn't mean to hurt you, but you've got to believe me - I was trying to do something *good*. Rock Star's really cool, mum. Dave too. And Tiny Tom, and Cheryl...'

'Tiny who?'

'Tiny Tom, he's the security guard that threw Mark Dooley out. He looks all tough with his gold teeth and everything but he's not. He watches Disney films! Cheryl's great, she even saved Rock Star's life. She's amazing at darts and pool. Dave's brilliant, he knows so much about gardening and stuff, and he can fix anything.' Freddie paused. 'Mum, you should see the rest of the mansion...'

Freddie's mum laughed awkwardly. 'As if that's going to happen! Something tells me I won't be going there, or anywhere, anytime soon - especially now Rock Star knows what you've been feeding him – *and* his guests. It's happening all over again, isn't it? Everyone's going to be pointing and laughing. It makes me feel sick just thinking about it.'

She put her hand to her mouth. 'Oh, Freddie. What have you done?'

CHAPTER 52 – THE CROWD

Freddie woke to the sound of the crowd outside his bedroom window and suddenly remembered everything that had happened the night before. All those people, staring straight at him. His stomach churned so much he felt like he was on a rollercoaster, only rollercoasters are supposed to be fun.

As the noise outside grew louder, Freddie swung his feet out of bed and listened. He crept over to the bedroom window, pulled back the corner of the curtain and waited for his eyes to adjust to the sunlight. He couldn't believe what he saw. There were people everywhere, filling the pavement in front of his house and all the way down the street. Instantly, cameras and hands started pointing up at his bedroom window and people were shouting his name.

He dropped the curtain as if he'd been given an electric

shock and perched back on the edge of his bed. All this upset, because of one crazy idea that had snowballed into something out of his control.

Looking at the sparkly bow tie on his bedroom carpet, last night's highlights flashed before his eyes. It was like watching a movie with all his favourite people in, but instead of them cheering his name and lifting him in the air to celebrate, they were all scowling at him and shaking their heads.

His poor mum. He'd let everyone down – his best friend, his gran, Rock Star – but it was his mum he'd hurt the most. At least Flash didn't understand what he'd done. Freddie shuffled down the bed to where his dog was sleeping and stroked his soft fur.

'You still like me, don't you?' asked Freddie quietly.

Flash replied by opening his eyes, breaking wind and facing the other way.

'Wow,' mumbled Freddie. 'You too'.

He wished he could go back in time and make it all right. He also wished he could open his window, because the smell that Flash had done was making his eyes water.

Freddie stared at the underwater scene that his mum had painted on his bedroom wall. For the first time ever, the great white shark with its mouth wide open seemed to be swimming straight for him. All he could think of were the last words his mum said to him.

'Oh, Freddie. What have you done?'

Freddie picked up the bow tie and threw it in the bin. 'Looks like I won't be needing that anymore,' he muttered. He climbed back into bed and pulled the duvet over his head.

CHAPTER 53 - PRISON

It had been two long days since Rock Star's dinner party and the crowd outside their home had finally got sick of waiting for something to happen. Peeking out through the curtains, Freddie could pretend that life had returned to normal - but he knew it hadn't.

His mum had shut herself away in her bedroom, and Freddie didn't have the faintest clue how to make everything better. He hated seeing her upset, especially knowing that it was all his fault. It was raining for the first time in ages, and the weather reflected his mood. Miserable. Freddie spent the morning in the front room, wishing he could jump into his mum's painting on the wall. He wanted to disappear onto that deserted beach and never come back.

That afternoon, Dylan crept in through the open back door

looking for signs of life. He found Freddie on his hands and knees on the kitchen floor. He'd been given the job of cleaning the cupboard under the sink, and it wasn't pleasant. So far, he'd found a large dead spider and something that used to be a potato, but now looked more like a plant.

'Hi mate,' said Dylan, 'mum said I could pop round to see how you're doing. Between you and me, I think she wants to know if there's any gossip... or if you'd been murdered and buried in the *nedrag*!'

Dylan took the chocolate bar out of his back pocket and offered half to Freddie, who removed his bright yellow rubber gloves and joined him at the table.

'It's horrible. Mum's hardly said two words to me. I made her favourite curry last night, *and* cake, and she hardly touched it. She said I'll probably have a moustache by the time I'm allowed out again.'

'You'll look like my mum then!' said Dylan, looking over at the cake. 'Have you heard anything from Rock Rats?'

'Nope. Nada. Zilch.'

Dylan let out a long sigh. 'Tickle a tarantula, I'll be gutted if this is the end of it all. I used to love going up there. Rock Rats has got more gadgets than Amazon! That pool table with the shrinking pockets was amazing, *and* the moving dartboard, and not forgetting my favourite, the ice cream jukebox...'

'I know, I know,' said Freddie, 'if you're trying to make me feel better it's not working. All I want to do is disappear. Mum's devastated, gran probably wants to karate chop me to death, and Rock Star? I dread to think how he's feeling after finding out he's been drinking my mum's sock juice for weeks. Not only that, he's fed it to all his guests too!' Freddie tilted his head to one side. 'Dylan, am I too young to go to prison?'

'Dunno,' Dylan replied, still looking at the cake, 'but look on the bright side. If you do end up in the slammer, prisons have got *huge* kitchens! You'd be able to cook potatoes all day long!'

Freddie walked over to the kitchen worktop and cut Dylan a large slice of cake. 'Here you go, mate. At least you'll enjoy it.'

The loud knock on the front door startled them both.

Dylan grabbed the cake, patted his friend on the shoulder and ran straight out of the kitchen door. 'Cheers for the *ekac*! Hang on in there, mate!'

Freddie swallowed and walked nervously down the hallway towards the front door. The hall had never felt so long, and his legs had never felt so heavy. He opened the door slowly, peering through the small gap. It was Dave, but something was different. Someone was standing behind him.

'Rock Star?' Freddie couldn't believe his eyes. 'What are you doing here?'

'Hi Freddie,' Dave replied, 'Rock Star wants to have a little chat with you, and your mum too if she's around?'

Freddie's mum stood at the top of the landing with her arms folded. 'Who is it?'

Freddie swung the door open. By the time his mum made it halfway down the stairs she didn't need an answer.

CHAPTER 54 – SWEATY LITTLE SUCKERS

Rock Star walked into the kitchen. His eyes shifted straight to the New York skyline painted on the wall. Taking in the scene for a minute, he sat down at the head of the kitchen table and leaned back in the chair. They'd never had anyone famous in the house before, and suddenly the kitchen looked very small. Freddie wasn't used to seeing him look serious. He looked like a judge about to hand out his punishment.

Freddie's mum decided to delay the judge's sentence by making drinks. Freddie sat down at one side of the table, Dave at the other. Everyone stared at the kettle which seemed to be taking a painfully long time to boil. Nobody was making eye contact.

Rock Star tapped his fingers on the table. 'We're waiting for one more person. If I remember rightly, she has her tea extra strong with one sugar.'

'That's how gran has it!' said Freddie, looking over at his mum.

Right on time, Freddie's gran burst into the kitchen. She was dressed in her gardening clothes and didn't look too impressed at being summoned.

'What's going on?' she asked, removing her gloves and sitting at the other end of the table from Rock Star. She looked everywhere but at the chair opposite.

'I haven't got a clue,' Freddie's mum replied, passing Rock Star a cup of tea. 'but before you start, Mr Rock Star - Sid - I'd like to apologise. I honestly had *no* idea what Freddie was up to.' She joined Freddie at his side of the table. 'If I'd have known, I'd have put a stop to this whole thing straight away.'

Rock Star nodded and raised his hand. 'Thanks for the apology, Kate, but it really isn't necessary. That boy of yours is one in a million.' He looked directly at Freddie. 'Bringing me that first batch of vegetable soup was very kind, and whatever happens from here, I'll always be very grateful.'

Freddie managed half a smile and a nod in Rock Star's

direction. He was so nervous he thought his heart was going to burst out of his chest.

Rock Star took a sip of his hot black tea and cleared his throat. 'Right then, I'll get straight to the point. After the dinner party, some of the guests started getting in touch with us.'

Freddie's face dropped. He looked at his mum who had turned very pale. She took Freddie's hand in her own and squeezed it tightly before replying in a tiny voice. 'I knew it. Are they going to sue us?'

'Sue?' replied Rock Star, nearly choking on his drink. 'Good heavens, not at all! Quite the opposite, in fact. They're all desperate to get their hands on some more! Your Rock Stock seems to be having the same effect on them too, and that's after just one bowl of the stuff!'

'Really?' asked Freddie.

'*Really?*' asked his mum.

Rock Star put his cup down. 'Absolutely! Kate, I know you're embarrassed about this whole situation, but you genuinely shouldn't be. *Your* smelly feet are your prized possession! In fact, if I was you, I'd insure them for millions! You've got something extremely special there, girl. You should be proud of those sweaty little suckers!'

'*Sweaty little suckers*?' she repeated, her eyes as big as dinner plates. She gazed around the table. Everyone sat perfectly still, not knowing how she was going to react. From out of nowhere she started laughing and Freddie sighed with relief.

Rock Star put his mug down and looked across the table at Freddie. 'Young man, with your cooking skills and your mum's smelly feet, you guys are *seriously* onto a winner. That's why I'd like to make you both a deal. Come up to my place tomorrow morning and I'll tell you all about it.'

'Can we, mum?' asked Freddie, ready to burst with excitement.

CHAPTER 55 – BEHIND BARS

His mum was smiling for the first time in days.

'I don't know what to say! Thanks, Rock Star. We'll be there.'

Rock Star turned to Freddie. 'You might want to use the secret tunnel, Freddie. There's TV crews camped out at the front gate.'

'Secret tunnel?' asked a confused Kate.

Freddie smiled and gave his mum a wink.

'By the way, Kate, I nearly forgot!' added Rock Star, 'I spoke to your old boss Marie Dooley at The Pockbury Times. I told her about how her son Mark Dooley had been blackmailing me, and she was horrified. She sacked him on the spot and called the police. Turns out he was blackmailing a few other people too. They've charged him this morning and he's on his way to jail right now. Sounds like he'll be behind bars for a *very* long time! Marie's taking over as manager again. She's even offered you your old job back, if you want it - although you might want to hear what I've got to offer tomorrow first.'

Freddie's mum squealed. 'Rock Star, I could kiss you!'

'If you don't mind, I've got a better idea,' blushed Rock Star. 'Is there any chance you can let Freddie use your socks? I've run out of Rock Stock, and I'm starving!'

Freddie held his breath, not knowing how his mum would react. Turning to him with a smile, she leaned over and ruffled Freddie's hair. He'd missed that.

Rock Star finished his drink and stood up. 'One last thing before I go. Freddie, do you mind if I borrow your gran for a quick word in the garden?' He looked directly over at the woman sat opposite him. 'What do you say, Shirl?'

His gran looked startled. She looked over at Freddie and opened her mouth as if she was going to say one of her witty remarks, but nothing came out. She gave a little nod, then walked straight outside with her head held high. She marched down to her son's old vegetable patch and folded her arms.

Rock Star walked over and stood next to her, kicking the ground like an awkward teenager.

'Shirley, I owe you a big apology. I didn't *not* invite you to the dinner party, if that makes sense. I honestly thought you'd moved away years ago. When I saw the names of the guests, I just thought you were Freddie's gran. Different surname, see.'

She unfolded her arms. 'I got married, Sid. I waited a whole year for you, but you didn't come back. Then I met my lovely Len. We had a fantastic life together. I've got no regrets, Sid. I'm happy.'

Rock Star gave her a cheeky smile. 'I can tell you're happy alright, I mean, just look at you! You've also got one heck of a karate kick on you too! Can you let me know who teaches you? I'm after some classes myself.'

Freddie's gran laughed. 'Funny you should say that!'

The Pockbury Times

FREE FOR POCKBURY RESIDENTS   **WRITTEN BY MARIE DOOLEY**

ROCK STAR
WORLD EXCLUSIVE
EXCITING CHANGES ALL ROUND

The events of Rock Star's dinner party sent shockwaves around the world. The secret ingredient of Rock Stock, sock juice, left many guests angry and upset - until they started to feel the benefits for themselves. With celebrities desperate to get their hands on more of the super-soup, the musician has set up **The Rock Stock Soup Co** with new business partner Kate Wilson and son Freddie.

On a visit to Rock Star's mansion, Kate told us: "The health benefits have sent demand through the roof. Thanks to my website, Soul Mates, I know many people with extremely smelly feet. These super-sweaters now join us every weekend to stay at our exciting new health club, **Star's Spa**.

They're picked up in Rock Star's supercars before joining in with the **fantastic facilities** on offer.

"Once they're hot and sweaty they soak their feet in our specially designed footbaths, or as we call them, **flavour tubs**. The flavour tub juice is sent to the kitchen where Freddie turns it into 'Rock Stock'. Each batch is numbered for customers to choose from. It's like picking a bottle of posh wine, only this is more expensive!"

Kate explained how life-changing this has been: "I used to be embarrassed by what made me different. Now I embrace it. My artwork is flying out too! After many requests, I splatter the paint with my socks and I can't keep up with demand!"

Locals can also enjoy Star's Spa for free, in return for a **random act of kindness**. Dave, Rock Star's right-hand man, told us more. "We've got tennis lessons, swimming lessons and karate classes. Tiny Tom runs a craft club, and Cheryl gives pool and darts lessons in Star's Bar."

BONITA BARRETT

The Pockbury Times

FREE FOR POCKBURY RESIDENTS　　WRITTEN BY MARIE DOOLEY

Rock Star's new business, Star's Spa, run with his new business partner Kate Wilson and her talented son Freddie

Dave also organises the park runs and looks after the huge allotment where they grow all the ingredients for the Rock Stock soup - except the footwear, of course!

Even Freddie's best friend Dylan is in on the action. "I get to film everything that happens here for my YouTube channel. Yesterday I received my gold YouTube play button plaque for having **one million subscribers**, which is brilliant - but it doesn't taste as nice as the *ekac* one that Freddie made me!"

So what does young chef Freddie make of it all? The 12-year-old told us: "**I'm living the dream**! Last week, Rock Star arranged for me to spend the day with the MasterChef judges. It was the best day of my life!"

Finally, we caught up with Rock Star who is looking **better than ever**. The world famous rocker told us more. "This all started with one boy's random act of kindness - and look what it's turned in to! I feel amazing, I've never been happier, and the best bit of all for me has been meeting up again with Freddie's gran, Shirley - the **love of my life**!"

Rock Star finished the interview with some exciting news for our readers. "Mark Dooley said I was more *gastric band* than *rock band*. That really hurt, but I liked the name. So, after Mark Dooley went to prison I contacted my old band mates and asked them if they'd like to reform - as **The Gastric Band**! Every month we'll be performing to guests and locals for free, right here on the steps of my mansion. **Rock on, Pockbury**!"

CHAPTER 56 - CHRISTMAS

Freddie made his way back from checking the turkey, with the Christmas music growing louder as he walked down the hall. The Christmas tree in the corner was a tenth of the size of the one in Rock Star's mansion, but here in his front room filled with his favourite people, it couldn't have been more perfect. He smiled as he saw the familiar couple standing directly under the mistletoe in the doorway. The familiar couple were his mum... and Dave.

'Knock it off,' said Freddie's gran, taking off her new night vision goggles, 'you'll wear the mistletoe out!'

The goggles were a gift for his gran so they could play their games of hide and seek in her garden all year round.

Freddie's mum walked over to her son, ruffled his hair and looked around the room smiling.

'Well, this is a little bit different from last Christmas!'

'The turkey's certainly bigger,' replied Freddie. 'Just as well too. Have you seen how much Dylan's mum eats?'

They both looked over to the sofa, where Dylan's mum was *enjoying* the large tin of chocolates. Some of the caramel filling was hanging from her moustache and it was wiggling every time she breathed in. Dylan's parents were unsurprisingly wearing matching Christmas jumpers, and unfortunately for Dylan, that included him too.

Rock Star tapped one of the Christmas tree decorations with the side of his glass. 'Right guys, it's present time. I hope you like them!' He held three shiny gold envelopes in his hand. They were addressed to Dylan, Freddie's gran, and Freddie.

Dylan went first. Rock Star had treated him and his parents to a trip to Hollywood, where a famous director was going to drive them round the studios in Dylan's dream car – a bright blue McLaren. Dylan was also going to be able to film the lot for his YouTube channel, including interviews with Hugh Jackman and Ryan Reynolds. Dylan's mum was so excited she dropped the chocolates.

'Hug a hedgehog!' yelled Dylan, punching the air. 'Thanks, Rock Rats!'

Freddie's gran went next. Inside the envelope was an old film stub for 'Easy Rider', the first film they saw together 50 years ago.

'Oh, Sid! You kept it!' said Freddie's gran, her eyes sparkling. 'I had no idea!' She looked up to see Rock Star waving some keys in the air.

'How about we have our own road trip, Shirl? I was thinking Route 66 on a pair of those big American choppers if you're up for it?'

The squeal of excitement and tight hug gave him the answer. When she finally let Rock Star out of her grip, he passed the last of the envelopes to Freddie.

'It's a trip around your house, but in real life. Happy Christmas guys!'

Freddie looked at his mum and Dave, who were just as confused. Inside the envelope were four postcards.

'I know you've not been on holiday for years,' said Rock Star, 'so I've arranged a month-long holiday of a lifetime for the three of you. You'll start in your 'kitchen' with a stay in New York, before heading off to your 'front room' to sit under a palm tree in Jamaica. From there, you'll spend a week in your 'bathroom' checking out the jungles of Brazil, and you'll finish with a trip to 'Freddie's bedroom' where you can explore Australia and the Great Barrier Reef. It's about time the three of you had some fun!'

Freddie launched himself at Rock Star, quickly followed by his mum and Dave. Rock Star found himself being hugged and thanked in three different directions and he enjoyed every second.

At the end of the hug, Freddie looked across at his gran. She smiled and winked.

'Rock Star,' said Freddie, '*We've* got a present for you, too. It's from all of us. We hope you like it!'

CHAPTER 57 - THE PRESENT

Rock Star's eyes lit up. He checked under the tree, but there was nothing there. He looked at Freddie and tilted his head. 'Now it's *my* turn to be confused!'

Freddie and Dylan both took his hands and led him through to the kitchen, where a large, wrapped present was waiting. It was nearly as wide as the New York skyline behind it. Rock Star walked over to it and smiled.

'Is this for me?' he asked excitedly.

The nods and giggles told him everything he needed to know. Rock Star ripped at the paper like an excited child, and as the last of the wrapping paper fell to the floor, he stared at the large brown box in front of him.

'A brown box! Thanks, guys! It's what I've always wanted!'

'I wish you'd told us that earlier,' said Freddie's gran, her

Christmas earrings flashing in time with the music. 'It would have saved us a fortune!'

Rock Star pulled the tape and the sides of the box fell away. There, in all its glory, was a shiny new dairy-free ice cream jukebox.

'Is this what I think it is?' asked Rock Star, his bottom lip starting to tremble.

Freddie smiled. 'It certainly is!'

'Your very own *xobekuj maerc eci*!' exclaimed Dylan.

'That's easy for you to say!' laughed Dave.

Freddie stood next to Rock Star. 'Your favourite ice cream flavours, but these ones are dairy free! They're all there – kebab flavour, pizza flavour, fish and chip flavour – and a couple of special editions for today. Christmas dinner flavour and Christmas pudding flavour, so we can all eat together. We know it's not the same as a *real* Christmas dinner...'

'It's better,' blurted Rock Star, his eyes filling with tears. 'I can't remember the last time I was given something so thoughtful. Thanks guys.'

Rock Star turned away from everyone for a moment and put

his hands up to his face. When he turned around, it was obvious he'd been crying. 'Last Christmas I thought I had everything, and when I came out of hospital, I realised I had nothing - or at least, nothing that really mattered. Don't get me wrong, all my stuff is cool, but that's all it is. *Stuff.*'

Rock Star walked over to Freddie's gran and placed a gentle kiss on her cheek.

'Having people that care about you, that's what matters. I feel like I've been given a family for Christmas, and that's the best present of all.'

Rock Star wiped a tear away with the back of his hand and looked over in Freddie's direction. 'Happy Christmas, Freddie.'

The smile on Freddie's face said everything.

THE END

ACKNOWLEDGEMENTS

Thank you to my talented friend and author Emma Garcia. From running through the basics of a character's arc, to reading early drafts, her insight has been invaluable.

On a personal level, I owe a huge thank you to my mum Shirley (who the cool gran is based on). She's always believed in my ability to do anything I set my mind to, but especially writing - and for that I am truly grateful. My best friend Michelle has been a very useful sounding board too, especially as an ex-teacher. I'm also extremely grateful to family and friends who have read this at different stages and have offered such enthusiasm and words of kindness.

Finally, in a theatrical Oscars-style, I'd like to thank my long-suffering husband Simon who has shared his wife with these characters for so long now. He'll be thrilled to hear he can have me back... for a while.

ABOUT THE AUTHOR

From writing short stories at school, to moody teenage poetry, to making up elaborate bedtime tales for her children, Bonita has always had an overactive imagination. As a child born in the 1970's, Bonita dreamt of three things – writing a book (in the hope of becoming the next Roald Dahl), dating a pop star (ideally Morten Harket from A-ha) and being a perfect size 10 forever (no matter how much chocolate she ate). None of these went entirely to plan.

Becoming disabled in her forties was certainly a twist in her storyline. Faced with a different pace of life, Bonita decided to dust off her distant childhood dream and start writing. She dived headfirst into a scary blank Word document, armed with nothing more than strong pain killers and a large bar of Cadbury Dairy Milk. Calling on first-hand experience, she wanted to write about how easy it is to hide away from the world when something doesn't go to plan - and the importance of repainting your wings and learning to fly again.

Approaching her half century, Bonita is finally achieving one of her three childhood dreams. This, her first book.

Printed in Great Britain
by Amazon